FIGHTING CHANCE

FIGHTING CHANCE

Ten Feet to Survival

Arthur Robinson
Gary North

American Bureau of Economic Research
Ft. Worth, Texas

Copyright © 1986
Arthur Robinson and Gary North

ISBN 0-930462-10-6
Library of Congress Catalog Card Number 86-71490

Typesetting by Thoburn Press, Tyler, Texas

Published by
American Bureau of Economic Research
P.O. Box 8204
Ft. Worth, Texas 76124

We dedicate this book to our
families and to the many Americans
whose foresight and courage have given us
freedom. We trust in God to give our generation
the wisdom to preserve that freedom.

TABLE OF CONTENTS

APPENDIXES

INTRODUCTION

Everyone knows that civil defense is boring. Civil defense is bomb shelters and stored food and medical kits. Civil defense doesn't have laser weapons, or satellites in outer space, or even guerrilla warfare. Hollywood isn't going to make a movie about a teenage computer whiz who breaks into a civil defense computer and nearly starts World War III. Civil defense doesn't have a computer to break into.

Yes, civil defense is boring. It's boring until the day the air raid sirens sound, and you finally ask yourself the 64-billion-dollar question: "What do we do now?"

It's obvious what you'd do *today* if the warning is real and there really are 10,000 Soviet nuclear warheads on the way. *You would probably die.* You would die because America doesn't have any civil defense. It also doesn't have any anti-missile defense. All we have is the threat of nuclear retaliation against the enslaved people behind the Iron Curtain, and even that threat is no longer believable, as you'll see when you finish this book. *We have no defense against a nuclear attack.* As one military expert on a U.S. Senator's staff admitted to one of the authors in 1984, "We couldn't stop an atomic attack even if the Soviets were using only cargo planes and rolling the bombs out the hatches."

Americans are undefended.

Most Americans assume either that civil defense takes care of itself somehow, or else they assume that it's not needed any more. They may vaguely remember the "bomb shelter" scare of the early 1960s, but they believe that whatever it was that scared us back then has been taken care of. Or they may think that a nuclear war will end the world, so it's useless to think about civil defense. Neither assumption is true. First, the thing that scared us in 1962 during the Cuban missile crisis is vastly more threatening today; second, a nuclear war won't end the world. But if the missiles fly before we get a civil defense shelter system, it will end *part* of the world: ours.

Twenty-eight percent of the world's population has civil defense shelters including the residents of Switzerland, China, and the Soviet Union. American citizens have none. Therefore, three and a half centuries of American history could end thirty minutes after the Soviet general staff pushes a few buttons.

And we are here to tell you, *it doesn't have to happen.* There *is* a way to change the catastrophic outcome.

The civil defense shelters recommended in this book would also protect the American people from fallout from nuclear power plant accidents, tornados, future chemical or biological accidents or warfare, and some types of terrorist threats. The Russian nuclear power plant accident at Chernobyl in May of 1986 is a most timely reminder that, even in the absence of war, civilian protection is important. Insurance against accidents and natural and terrorist threats justifies a civilian shelter system. The Soviet military threat, however, justifies it 1000 times over.

Many well-meaning people have sought refuge from the Soviet threat in arms control treaties with the Soviets. The U.S. has obeyed the terms of those treaties, and the Soviets have repeatedly violated them. Those treaties have merely served to worsen the threat that we face.

When good and evil are placed in opposition to one another, good usually triumphs over evil. However, when good and evil make pacts with one another, it is usually evil which triumphs. We should not hate the Soviets and certainly not the Russian, Asian, and Eastern European people whom they have enslaved. But we *must* realize that they are in the hands of evil, that they will act accordingly, and that we must be prepared.

Arthur Robinson and Gary North
June 1986

Part I
THE PROBLEM

1

THE MYTHS WE LIVE
(AND MAY DIE) BY

Today, the American people are completely undefended against Soviet attack. We have no air defense, no missile defense, and no civil defense. We have been told by our military strategists that we are being defended by the threat of vengeance—by our missiles' ability to kill the Soviet people *after* their missiles have killed us. This, however, is not true. By means of anti-aircraft defenses, anti-missile defenses, civil defense, and a first-strike military doctrine, the Soviets have become nearly invulnerable to any American attack. Their defenses have also been strengthened by the fact that our offensive weapons have become obsolete and many have been dismantled.

We spend $300 billion on our military each year. Less than one year of that budget would build a formidable civil defense and strategic defense with off-the-shelf technology—now. Less than 10% of that budget each year would support the research, development, and deployment of advanced strategic defense systems—later. We need *defense*—now and later. At present, we are wasting most of that $300 billion each year, assuming that remaining vulnerable year after year to a Soviet first strike constitutes wasted defense money. We are defenseless. So are our soldiers and our sailors.

The United States, our civilization, and our children and grandchildren could easily perish if we do not immediately defend ourselves. We must build a civil defense and a strategic defense. We must also build a *defense of truth* against the myths about nuclear war. These myths have led, in part, to our present predicament.

There is a lot of confusion in people's minds about the realities of nuclear war. As a nation, we have hope in things that are hopeless, and we mistrust things that are trustworthy. Let us begin with a discussion of some false hopes.

Myths About Military Defense

There are several important myths that many Americans believe concerning the military power of the United States. It is understandable why we believe in them. We have lived in peace within our borders since the Civil War. Destructive wars are what *other* nations experience. We assume that this peace has been the product of our military might. Since we have long had internal peace within our borders, we assume that we will still have sufficient military power to protect us.

We can list the myths of American military defense:

1. "Peace is the absence of domestic invasion."
2. "Peace is the product primarily of military power."
3. "If no one is shooting, there is peace."
4. "The Soviets talk conquest, but that's just rhetoric for the people back home. They have always talked conquest, but they don't mean it any more."
5. "Both sides have enough weapons to destroy each other five times over."
6. "The Soviets regard nuclear war as irrational and unthinkable."
7. "Nuclear war *is* unthinkable."
8. "Nobody can win a nuclear war."
9. "After a nuclear war, the survivors will envy the dead."
10. "Soviet military weapons are of poor quality and will not work properly."
11. "The United States has a defense system (other than massive retaliation) against atomic attack."

These are false myths. They are very dangerous to the survival of our civilization and ourselves. Each of these is considered in the chapters of this book. First, let us consider the myth of American defense.

In the written draft of the speech that he did not live to deliver in Dallas, President Kennedy devoted considerable space to the new high-technology nuclear weapons that the United States possessed. He mentioned our conventional forces. He promised massive retaliation against any aggressor. But his closing words were the official foundation of his military doctrine.

> We, in this country, in this generation, are —by destiny rather than choice—the watchmen on the walls of world freedom. We ask, therefore, that we may be worthy of our power and responsibility, that we may exercise our strength with wisdom and restraint, and that we may achieve in our time and for all time the ancient vision of peace on earth, good will toward men. That must always be our goal—and the righteousness of our cause must always underlie our strength. For as was written long ago, "Except the Lord keep the city, the watchman waketh but in vain."

He was quoting from Psalm 127:1. The entire verse reads: "Except the Lord build the house, they labor in vain that build it: except the Lord keep the city, the watchman waketh but in vain."

Our weakness today is startling. President Kennedy's last speech is like some ancient parchment from a long-dead world. It no longer rings true. Our weapons are ineffective. We are no longer able to serve as the watchman of world freedom. The cause of our decline is moral and spiritual. We have become the watchmen who wake in vain. Worse: we are watchmen who are still asleep, while our nation is in mortal peril.

The prevailing strategy of American nuclear defense is simple: if the Soviets launch an attack on us, we will retaliate. We have dismantled every other defensive device. Only this threat remains: "You nuke us, and we'll nuke you." It has been official policy—the *only* policy—for over 20 years. It is also hopeless, ineffective, and immoral. It worked only for as long as the Soviets had not built up their defenses and their first-strike capability. It took the Soviets 20 years to overcome our previous strength. The risk-reward ratio of a first strike against the U.S. is dropping steadily for the Soviets, year after year: more reward, less risk.

The U.S. retaliation policy has a name: Mutual Assured Destruction. Better yet, it has an acronym: MAD. This is a good description of the policy. In order to "save money" and "reduce the arms race," strategic planners in the 1960s came up with the idea that if each side really could annihilate the other side's entire population, then both sides could stop producing weapons once destruction was assured.

What this really meant was that each side's military forces were supposed to keep as hostages the other side's civilian population. The word "hostages" was never used, of course. That would have exposed the policy as the monstrous crime that it is. Military tradition throughout history has been clear: warriors should target warriors. Since World War II, however, strategic planners have been deliberately targeting civilians. It is a devilish policy.

It was also a preposterous policy from the beginning. Why should the Soviet Union be content with a stalemate? They are Communists. Marxism-Leninism is inherently, self-consciously expansionist. They are an empire—an "evil empire" as President Reagan used to say. They want more. As some humorist once said, "The policy of the Soviet Union is simple. They want every piece of land that touches their borders, so their borders never stop expanding."

The Soviets didn't stop. They keep expanding—directly (Afghanistan) and indirectly through client states—and they also keep building weapons of mass destruction. The fifth generation of missiles, the SS-24 to SS-28 series, is coming off the assembly lines now. These are mobile missiles that cannot be targeted by our fixed-base missiles. Their missiles can destroy our easily targeted missiles, but ours are not able to destroy their new ones.

As we will show in the following chapter, their deliverable intercontinental ballistic missile warheads outnumber ours by a very large margin. Yet even this is misleading: they have anti-missile defenses, while we don't. They have a strategy of a first strike in their plans; we don't. Our moral values do not permit a first strike and, in any case, we don't have enough deliverable warheads to destroy the bulk of their warheads in a first strike. They have a civil defense; we don't.

Therefore, we cling to a policy of mutual assured destruction, but we don't have the power to implement it. The public knows little about this policy, but those few who understand it and also believe in it have been misled. They are putting their faith in a will-o'-the-wisp. They are exercising faith in a policy that was dead a decade ago.

The main myth of American military defense is that we are being defended. We are not being defended. The policy that supports our entire military bureaucracy and costs about $300 billion a year does not defend us. We are no longer able to inflict any significant damage on the Soviet Union compared to the lethal damage they can inflict on us. Thus, there is no serious deterrent.

But we're still a free people. If we aren't being defended, then why don't the Soviets invade, or bomb us into oblivion? We offer two answers. First, *they may be about to do so. That's why we desperately need a workable civil defense system.* Second, they are champion chess players. They take no unnecessary risks. The elite Soviet leaders want to win without any serious risks to their wealth and power, no matter how temporary. If the Soviet warheads don't strike us today, it isn't because MAD works; it's because they are sufficiently successful against us without taking any major military risks at all. They are winning "on the cheap."

They think they can bide their time. They avoid direct confrontations, so as to keep the American people asleep. This policy has worked ever since the 1962 Cuban missile crisis. They also continue to build nuclear warheads and missiles beyond any level that makes sense if their goals were strictly defensive. They are patient. They are not asleep. *We* are asleep.

In 1973, Soviet Premier Leonid Brezhnev announced:

By 1985, we will be able to extend our will wherever we wish.[1]

There is little evidence today that his forecast was incorrect.

Myths About Civil Defense

Nuclear war. Because this book is about this grim topic, a lot of people may toss it aside. But for those who want to face reality, the facts of nuclear war cannot safely be ignored. The facts can be ignored, of course: just not safely.

What is the reality of nuclear war? Before we consider this question in a little more detail, we need to know what *isn't* true about nuclear war. We need to know the myths. These include the following:

---

1. Cited in Quentin Crommelin, Jr. and David S. Sullivan, *Soviet Military Supremacy* (Washington, D.C.: Citizens Foundation, 1985), p. 27.

1. "Nobody could survive an air burst nuclear explosion directly overhead at maximum destruction height."
2. "Few living creatures would survive an all-out atomic attack on the United States, except in very rural areas."
3. "The modern world would be bombed back into the Dark Ages; it would take a thousand years to rebuild."
4. "Civil defense is impractical and incredibly expensive. That's why no nation ever spends much money on civil defense."

Every one of these "facts" is a myth. These myths are false. The truth is that:

1. No *unprotected* person could survive a blast overhead at optimum burst height, but virtually 100% of those inside properly designed shelters could survive if they had as little as ten extra feet of dirt and a properly designed shelter in between them and the blast.
2. Most living creatures would survive if they were over five miles from a blast, assuming the bombs had been exploded above-ground (not much fallout). Even with extensive fallout, our natural environment of plants and animals would be re-established within a few years.

3. People with knowledge and faith are what make an economy, not buildings. If most of the population could get into bomb shelters before an attack, then America's crucial resource would survive: people.

4. The Soviets today have enough nuclear weapons to kill over 90% of the U.S. population, because America has no bomb shelters. The U.S. could not kill more than 5% of the Soviet population, because they do have shelters, and they also have a strategic defense. They spend the equivalent of about $40 billion a year on shelters, the actual deployment of anti-ballistic missiles and radars, and "star wars" research.

5. The Soviet Union has published its military strategy repeatedly, and it is based on the legitimacy, efficiency, and strategic necessity of a nuclear first strike against the U.S.

6. The United States has no defense system at all. None. The entire "defense" strategy is based on nuclear retaliation *after* a Soviet nuclear attack. Even that retaliatory threat is no longer backed by credible military ability.

7. Excellent civil defense systems already protect 28% of the world's population: Soviet citizens, Red Chinese citizens, and the Swiss.

And then there is the reassuring but highly unlikely myth that's so popular with America's strategic
planners:

"The Soviets don't target civilians."

If anyone remarks to you that the Soviets don't
target civilians, just reply: "Tell it to Afghanistan.
Tell it to the heirs of the 20 million to 30 million of
their own citizens that Stalin murdered or starved,
1928-1941.[2] Tell it to the Soviet military officials who
are sitting on top of at least 10,000 (or more) *deliverable* nuclear warheads, plus airplane-carried bombs."
(Do you think there are 10,000 *military* targets in the
West?)

Finally, "Tell it to the relatives of the 269 passengers of Korean Airlines flight 007."

There is an absolutely basic military rule:

*"Act according to the enemy's capability; never act
according to what you think his intentions and goals
are."*

What is our enemy's capability? As long as we
lack a civil defense, the Soviet capability is to kill
90% of our people in a first strike. Their strategic
and civil defense systems, based upon our own original research and designs, make them immune to
counterattack.

---

2. Robert Conquest, *The Great Terror* (New York: Holt, Rinehart & Winston, [1968] 1973), p. 710.

There is agreement among our planners that the Soviets have adopted the strategy of a first strike on our *military* targets. There is also agreement that the Soviets would be unconcerned if that strike just happened to kill 50 or 100 million Americans as a side effect. There is disagreement, however, as to whether or not they would *intentionally* kill 200 million, since they may have confidence that they can subdue and subjugate us after a nuclear defeat. They subjugated the Russian people and subsequently many other nations.

As long as they have the *capability* to kill all of us and our families, then they can enslave all of us even without an attack. The Communists have repeatedly demonstrated on their own people and on civilians all over the world that they actually use mass murder whenever they believe it serves their interests.

Some Americans hold a belief that the Soviets intend to capture the productive power of America intact—that they would not destroy American factories and the American population. But, for the moment, put yourself in the place of these ruthless mass-murderers when they are faced with the following alternatives:

A. Assured success in their quest to achieve total world power at the expense of a temporary wasteland on the North American continent.

B. A counter-attack led by American survivors which might result in the disintegration of the Soviet Empire and the capture of Soviet leaders by their former slaves.

What do you really believe they will do? There may be other options open to them, but *are you willing to take the chance?* When the stakes are this high, we cannot afford to gamble. Unfortunately, our political leaders *are* gambling by refusing to build us a shelter system.

If you are still convinced that the present Soviet leadership would not order the annihilation of 90% of the American population, how can you be sure who will be in control of more than 10,000 weapons of mass destruction tomorrow — or next week? It is the nature of totalitarian regimes to experience continual power struggles, and the most ruthless contestants are the most likely winners.

We Deserve Protection

You and I can't do much about military strategy. The generals, admirals, and military strategists won't pay much attention to us. But we know enough to get in out of the nuclear rain. We can tell our elected representatives that we demand physical protection. Our problem is simple: the government is too busy spending our money on other things. No one has built any holes in the ground for us to "get into" during that kind of rain.

Holes in the ground. It's so obvious. The Soviets have them, the Red Chinese have them, and the Swiss have them. The rest of us don't. A properly designed steel case in a hole ten feet underground would keep alive practically everyone inside, even in an all-out atomic attack. The only exception: a direct hit by a ground-exploded bomb. Nevertheless, if all of the Soviet arsenal of nuclear weapons were exploded at ground level in the U.S., with the shelters as their actual targets, over 90 percent of everyone in the shelters would survive.

Ground-exploded bombs are aimed only at such targets as missile silos and airport runways. They are less than half as effective in knocking down structures than are air-exploded bombs. They create fallout, unlike air-exploded bombs, but properly designed shelters are immune to fallout. During the first one to three weeks, the fallout in most places would dissipate to safe levels.

The U.S. government could buy mass-produced shelters and install them ten feet underground for about $200 per person. An additional $100 per person will provide needed supplies for survival during the year after a major attack.

With the federal budget now at a trillion dollars a year, why can't the government spend at least $300 on every U.S. resident in order to give each American an excellent chance of surviving a nuclear attack and rebuilding the country? Why don't they at least try to give our families a fighting chance?

A fighting chance. Not a guarantee of everyone's survival, not a guaranteed way to end nuclear war forever (although it would drastically reduce the likelihood of a war), and not a way to make nuclear war a picnic, but a fighting chance of survival. Is that worth $300 apiece? Is it worth a letter or telegram to your Congressman and your two U.S. Senators to persuade them that it's worth $300 apiece?

Conclusion

Belief in myths and ignorance of facts has led our country to a dangerous and likely fatal position today. The facts, however, show us straightforward ways in which to correct this situation.

The amazing part is that these facts are for the most part 30-year-old facts. President Kennedy was aware of them. He wanted to set up a civil defense system a lot like the one we recommend here. But the voters were never told the simple facts that were available 30 years ago. They haven't been given a chance to make up their own minds. The American people not only haven't been given a fighting chance, they haven't even been given a chance to think rationally about a fighting chance.

2

UNILATERAL ASSURED DESTRUCTION

In November of 1985, the United States spent
$21 million to dismantle a Poseidon submarine. This
was done in order to "stay within the limits of the
SALT II treaty" that was never ratified by the U.S.
Senate and is therefore not a treaty. In the spring of
1986, President Reagan announced that he intended
to dismantle two more, for the same reason: "to go
the extra mile" with the Soviet Union. (How many
miles do we go before we walk over a cliff?)

What's going on here?

The facts in this chapter are known to very few
voters. If voters were aware of the information in
this chapter, they would be far more concerned
about their futures. They might begin to demand
national defense. We are paying $300 billion a year,
and we are not being defended.

Our leaders are following a policy of appeasement toward the Soviet Union. They are afraid to
defend us, even with the non-offensive methods of

civil defense and strategic defense, lest that defense might upset the Soviets. Instead our defense dollars are spent on bureaucracy, military pensions, offensive arms, and military adventures directed toward challenges that don't really threaten our survival.

After you have read this chapter, you'll understand why we are calling for immediate construction of a civil defense blast shelter system.

We are not apologists for the Pentagon. Our general assessment of all bureaucracies is that they live for their own sake, mainly to get fatter, and to feather the career nests of their employees, especially senior managers. A peacetime military establishment is one of the least reliable of all bureaucracies precisely because the general public really doesn't want to have its military prowess tested in the only meaningful way possible: a war. So of all bureaucracies, the military bureaucracies get fat. They also get slow.

Obviously, we need military defense. We know of no significant voting bloc or alignment that favors unilateral disarmament. But we aren't getting a nuclear defense with the hundreds of billions we are forced to pay each year. The fact is: *we are not presently defended from nuclear attack*.

Retired General Al Knight has reported that he has personally seen an air strip in Cuba capable of launching jets that can carry nuclear bombs. He has seen photographs of a second air strip. There are seven more, he says.

When he warned a senior military commander (now retired) of this threat, the man admitted that the United States has no AWACS radar observation planes to patrol the Cuban-U.S. air space. We sold them to the Arabs and to Europe (which really can't make good use of them). The commander admitted that he wanted several of them, but he couldn't get even one.

What's going on here?

Soviet military supremacy is not a popular topic these days. People don't want to think about it. But once in a while, we need to take inventory. We need to sit down and look at the balance sheet. In the field of military preparedness, it is an *imbalance sheet*. (In foreign policy, of course, it has been an imbalance sheet since the days of the Wilson Administration. But that's just our opinion. The statistics on today's military hardware are facts.)

Human history does not hinge exclusively on the number of "chariots" on two sides of a border. But *the decisions of policy-makers are highly influenced by the statistics of chariots*. This is why we need to be familiar with the numbers. The numbers will eventually have their effect on policy-makers.

Counting Chariots

Almost nobody in the United States Congress wants to talk about the present military imbalance. The public isn't told of the extent of this imbalance. Voters assume that the President has things under control. So let's look at the statistics. If you haven't seen any of this before, you're in for a shock. It is assumed by our strategists that MAD will work. It won't.

The problem is, both sides are no longer equally vulnerable. The Soviets are barely vulnerable, and with each month, they become less vulnerable. Their anti-ballistic missile program (ABM) and their civil defense program see to that. They have thereby defeated MAD. They don't actually have to launch that first strike; they only have to persuade our decision-makers that *they can* and that *they are willing to*.

The United States has adopted a defensive strategy based on *vengeance* rather than *defense*. This is what General Daniel Graham's High Frontier (strategic defense) supporters claim is the heart of our weakness. We cannot defend our civilian population. Even our anti-ballistic missile system of the early 1970s, which has been completely dismantled, was going to be used primarily to defend our own offensive (retaliatory) missiles, not civilian populations.

Soviet Anti-Ballistic Missiles

The Soviets have just about completed an anti-ballistic missile radar system. They have at least 7,000 operational radar units. According to reports which were given to us in 1985, they now have a new anti-missile defense system *in actual production* which can hit any of our missiles or planes as they approach Soviet targets with half a dozen or more missiles. We have developed the same technology, but *we have not deployed it.*

After a Soviet first strike nuclear attack, we would be so weak that a successful invasion of the U.S. could be launched from Cuba. We don't think about it because there's nothing we can do about it.

At present, there is no U.S. air defense system whatsoever.

The Nuclear Arsenals

According to Secretary of Defense Weinberger, writing in *Soviet Military Power*, March 1986, U.S. Department of Defense, the Soviets have developed a stock of ready-to-launch Intercontinental Ballistic Missles, (ICBMs), with over 6,000 deliverable warheads capable of destroying U.S. missle silos. These are first-strike offensive weapons. They also have about 3,000 ready-to-launch submarine-launched ballistic missle warheads and about 2,000 bomber-launched nuclear weapons.

This totals *11,000 nuclear weapons* that can be exploded by the Soviets over the United States in a *first strike today.* The delivery systems for these weapons are five years old or less.

Our Minuteman III missiles are about 15 years old on average.

Moreover, Crommelin and Sullivan, writing in *Soviet Military Supremacy*, estimate that the Soviets have about 800 sea launched cruise missiles and the capability of launching an *additional* 11,000 nuclear weapons by reloading their first-strike missile launchers.

If these estimates are correct, we now face a 20,000 nuclear explosion threat. Even if only the facts that Secretary Weinberger has revealed are considered, then the current threat is 11,000 warheads, and the Soviet rate of production means that we may face a 20,000 warhead threat in the near future. Secretary Weinberger would, for security reasons, be unlikely to speak publicly about the reload possibility.

Soviet military doctrine calls for a first strike on the United States without warning. The United States has about 1,000 fifteen-year-old ICBM's, about 40 ballistic missile submarines, and about 300 thirty-year-old B-52 intercontinental bombers. Only those 20 submarines that are at sea (half are in port at any given time) have much chance to survive a Soviet first strike. Even these 20 are continuously hunted by the Soviet navy and are becoming vulnerable to satellite detection systems which the Soviets are developing. They may not survive either.

Therefore, our 1,000 ICBM's, our 300 bombers, our 40 submarines, and our 500 surface ship navy can be destroyed by less than 20% of the Soviet first-strike force. Even if they use three warheads for every military target, they will still have over 5,000 nuclear weapons left over for other strategic and *civilian* targets. With possible reloads or with future deployments, this figure rises to 10,000 to 15,000.

We do not have any defense whatsoever against these weapons. We know how to deploy antiballistic missiles and civil defense systems that would protect us from this threat, *but we have deployed nothing.*

We have initiated a "Star Wars" advanced defense technology research program. Our program has much less funding than the similar Soviet program and is, according to Dr. Edward Teller, about 10 years behind the Soviet program.

It is estimated that, at best, less than 10% of our weapons could escape destruction and actually reach the Soviet Union. Moreover, those 10% could do little damage to the Soviets, who have deployed extensive civil defense and anti-missile defense systems.

In hope that something might get through, our missiles have been aimed at the suspected bomb shelters of Politburo members and some other "makes them nervous" targets. In response, the Soviets have hardened these shelters so thoroughly that extreme accuracy and luck would be necessary to damage them.

Over the past 20 years, the size of the U.S. nuclear arsenal has decreased by 30% and *the total megatonnage has dropped by 75%*. This trend would be expected from the increased efficiency of the weapons and accuracy of their delivery systems. The Soviet totals have, however, risen dramatically. They are still building. We aren't.

The average age of our missiles is 15 years. When the U.S. tried to launch two satellites with Titan missiles (the second one in the spring of 1986) they both blew up.

The U.S. has a fleet of B-52 bombers. They are flown by crew members who are much younger than the planes they fly. The B-52 is a plane designed in the late 1940s. Consider this: we are "defended" by the threat that we will retaliate with a fleet of bombers designed before the Korean War.

In June 1986 President Reagan announced that he planned to exceed the Salt II limits for deployment of cruise missiles on B-52's in December 1986. The administration is also deploying 50 MX missiles and a limited number of B1 bombers.

The MX and B1 are partially obsolete before deployment, since they have endured not only the usual bureaucratic delays in development but also a political delay. The government under the Carter administration refused to deploy them seven years ago. Moreover, these current deployment levels are dwarfed by the massive new Soviet systems currently being deployed.

Therefore, in June 1986, the United States is proceeding with limited, ineffective, new deployments of offensive weapons of retaliation in continuation of the failed and immoral MAD strategy of vengeance. No plans whatever are being made for *deployment* of either a strategic defense or a comprehensive civilian defense.

It is a fundamental military principle that the highest force level, in this case nuclear weapons, dominates the lower force levels. For example, the surface ships of an apparently strong navy can be easily eliminated by the higher force level of nuclear bombardment. For completeness, however, let's also look at the lower force comparisons.

Navy

How about the U.S. Navy? Here is the one area since 1980 where there has been considerable improvement. We used to have 1,000 ships. They were mostly put into mothballs. Here is the grim reality in 1985, after five years of improvement:

Chart 1

Can America Catch Up?

CHART 12
The Naval Balance (end of 1983)

	United States	Soviet Union
Aircraft Carriers	13	5
Battleships	2	0
Cruisers/Destroyers	98	107
Frigates	103	195
Ballistic Missile Submarines	35	79
Nuclear Attack Submarines	95	120
Diesel Attack Submarines	4	168
Amphibious Ships	61	177*
Patrol Combatants	6	455
Mine Warfare	3	339
Logistics and Support	105	772
Missile Craft	0	145
TOTAL	**525**	**2562**

*Includes 82 amphibious ships and 95 amphibious warfare ships.
Sources: *DOD Annual Report for FY 1985*; *Soviet Military Power 1984*; *Journal of Defense & Diplomacy*, January 1984; *Armed Forces Journal*, April 1984.

From *Can America Catch Up?*

The U.S. has built 27 attack submarines in the last ten years; the Soviets have built 61. From 1976 to 1983, the Soviets built 86 submarines, three times the U.S. production level. At the beginning of this year, we had 36 major nuclear subs on duty, but only half of which are at sea at one time. The Soviets have over 100 nuclear attack subs, and over 150 diesel subs (less of a threat). They have over 250 attack submarines total with which to trail our 18 that are at sea at any time.

Army

What about the Army? Not so good. The numbers are as follows:

Chart 2

Can America Catch Up?

CHART 5
The Military Manpower Balance 1983
Regular Forces and Reserves (thousands)

General Purpose Forces	U.S.	USSR
Army	780	1800
Navy	558	445*
Air Force	592	1290**
Marines	194	15
Paramilitary	103***	450
Total GPF	2227	4000
Reserves	1005	5000
Grand Total	3232	9000

*Excludes Naval Infantry (Marines).
**Includes Strategic Rocket Force (SRF), National Air Defense Troops (Voyska-PVO), and Aviation Armies.
***Coast Guard (active, reserve, and auxiliary) plus Civil Air Patrol.
Sources: *The Military Balance, 1983-84,* International Institute for Strategic Studies, London, 1983; Secretary of Defense, *Annual Report, FY 1985.*

From *Can America Catch Up?*

We have virtually no specialized forces in guerrilla warfare, which is a key form of combat in modern times. Here is where we are also losing—Latin America is within walking distance of El Paso.

Rapid Deployment Force

Then there is the so-called Rapid Deployment Force, now referred to as CENTCOM. So far, it lacks equipment. If it had *six weeks,* it could transport *one Army division* to the Middle East. The Soviets, according to Dr. Angelo Codevilla, can send 20 divisions into Iran, if necessary. When asked how much the Soviets can do in Iran and get away with it, he replied, "Anything they want to: they're the 400-

pound gorilla in the region."

Lt. Gen. Robert Kingston, the Commander-in-Chief of CENTCOM, said in 1984 that "the forces assigned are not as sustainable as they should be, nor will they be adequately sustained in the foreseeable future."

Could we support even a full-scale effort in the Middle East? One estimate concludes that 80% of the U.S. sealift fleet capacity would be absorbed by such an operation in the Persian Gulf.

We have 21 minesweepers, barely enough to clear more than two of our nation's dozen major port cities. We plan to build 25 more over the next four years. The Soviet Union has 380 minesweepers, one-third more than all NATO forces combined.

Here is the summary, U.S. versus the U.S.S.R.:

Chart 3

Can America Catch Up?

United States		Soviet Union
	Ground Combat Divisions	
16*		195
	Battle Force Ships	
524**		2,249
	Merchant Marine Ships	
12		1,800
	Attack Aircraft	
2,606		6,750
	Tanks	
4,960		51,900
	Armored Personnel Carriers	
7,090		63,390
	Artillery Tubes	
1,350		46,300

From *Crommelin & Sullivan*

Other Factors

Communications: We are totally dependent on our satellites for information and command. The Soviets have conducted at least *20 anti-satellite weapon tests involving the destruction of actual targets*. The first test was in 1968. We have no operational anti-satellite weapon.

Then there was the *neutron bomb*. We stress the word "was." It kills soldiers, not cities. A good weapon for European terrain. We developed it and built it, but we didn't deploy it. Too destructive, you understand. Why, it might *kill* people! People such

Chart 4

Can America Catch Up?

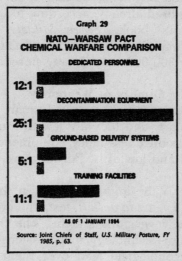

Graph 29

**NATO—WARSAW PACT
CHEMICAL WARFARE COMPARISON**

DEDICATED PERSONNEL

12:1

DECONTAMINATION EQUIPMENT

25:1

GROUND-BASED DELIVERY SYSTEMS

5:1

TRAINING FACILITIES

11:1

AS OF 1 JANUARY 1984

Source: Joint Chiefs of Staff, *U.S. Military Posture, FY 1985*, p. 63.

The lower, shorter bars represent the NATO resources of chemical agents.

From *Can America Catch Up?*

as invading Soviet tank crews.

But we've got the *cruise missile*, and they don't, right? Wrong. They've got a lot of them, and we are scrambling to catch up. We have ordered 1400 for the Navy, and we are installing cruise missiles on our 30-year-old B-52's.

Need we mention *civil defense*? We don't have any. Much of our economic production takes place in coastal cities. Most of the Soviet Union's production is far inland. A lot of their military production is underground.

The last area—potentially the most devastating —is *chemical and biological warfare*. The Soviets have a major production program.

The Soviets have 700,000 tons of chemical warfare agents stored already, according to Crommelin and Sullivan's book, *Soviet Military Supremacy.* NATO's estimate is lower. NATO estimates that the Soviets have 300,000 tons already stored.

Quality of Weaponry

What about our much-vaunted "smart weapons"? They are smart, and they are few in number. The Soviets do produce less fancy equipment, but they produce lots and lots of it. Furthermore, they steal our ideas.

But here is the important fact: in the U.S., it takes up to 15 years to design, test, and put into production a new weapons system. The Soviets can implement our technology much faster. Thus, our supposed technological lead over them is largely mythical, and our military leaders repeatedly testify to this. (By "our," we mean the U.S. and NATO; we are not speaking of the Israeli military, which does not labor under 15-year bureaucratic Defense Department procedures, and whose technological miracles are not easily stolen by the U.S.S.R.) Official testimony indicates that the Soviets have narrowed the technological gap in some areas from 8-10 years to 2-3 years. (Testimony of Admiral James Watkins, Chief of Naval Operations, before the Senate Armed Services Committee, 1984.)

Lt. Gen. James Merryman, the Army's Deputy Chief of Staff for Research, Development & Acquisition says: "The only area we rate ourselves as close to parity to the Soviets is field artillery. . . . If we went to war tomorrow, they not only outnumber us, but most of what they have as equipment is better." (*Defense Daily*, 22 Nov. 1983, p. 113.)

On June 10, 1984, we successfully demonstrated a spectacular new anti-missile defense system called the Homing Overlay Experiment (HOE) vehicle. It has been described as the technological equivalent of hitting a bullet in flight with another bullet. As soon as it was demonstrated, the program was *cancelled*. The HOE works, but it was intended as a research program, not as a defense system.

This is standard operating procedure with the military today. They respond with a *research program* to demands that America be defended. When the research is finished — if it is ever finished — the developed technology is not put into production and deployed.

A First Strike Against Civilians

American civilians are hostage to a Soviet attack; Soviet civilians are safe from American attack. The MAD doctrine is, therefore, defunct, and we remain alive solely at the pleasure of Soviet generals and politicians.

This overwhelming Soviet force can have only one purpose — the complete destruction of the United States. It can be used to:

1. Destroy our military and kill 90% of our people in a first strike.
2. Destroy our military in a first strike and then demand the surrender of our civilians.
3. Demand the surrender of our military and our civilians under threat of first strike.
4. Coerce our leaders into continual surrender to Soviet interests around the world and then the eventual domination of America and actual surrender.

Any one of these possibilities leads to the end of our civilization in the near future.

It is the authors' opinion that the first option (first-strike destruction of our military and civilians) will be chosen by the Soviets *unless* we build a defense, because:

1. Our productivity and example are embarrassments to the Soviets, who have an inferior economic system.
2. Our Judeo-Christian ethics and morals are

absolutely irreconcilable with Soviet tyranny.

3. The Soviets have built their vast military machine through great economic suffering and hardships imposed upon their people. Their military machine will age. They must use it or lose it.

4. We are capable of building a defense and an offense superior to theirs if we regain the will to do so. This danger threatens them as long as we exist.

The temptation to eliminate all of these problems in 30 minutes is very great for the Soviets. They have repeatedly shown in their own country and numerous other countries that *mass slaughter of civilians* (even their own) is done without hesitation when it serves their interests.

U.S. Defeat or Destruction?

An alternative thesis held by many strategic analysts is that the Soviets really want our productivity and not our destruction. Many thoughtful scientists who study the Soviet Union have concluded that the Soviets will not deliberately attack civilians. They have also concluded, however, that the Soviets would regard with indifference the possible deaths of 50 million or more Americans during a first strike upon the strategic military targets in the United States. The Soviets planned an attack on China in 1969 (see Chapter 3) that would have killed millions of unprepared Chinese, Japanese and other civilians with fallout. This aspect of the plan was a minor matter to them.

The suggestion that they want our productivity overestimates the concern of the Soviet elite for the lives of their slaves. Until now, they have needed American productivity in order to give an appearance of economic competence and in order to build their war machine. In a post-war world, however, the Soviet elitists will live in luxury and with absolute power regardless of whether industrial productivity is at a 1980s or a 1960s or even a 1940s level. The Soviet elite would not hesitate to return Soviet citizens even to the 1940s in exchange for absolute, unquestioned total world power.

There is one more consideration: *envy*. It's not simply that they would like our productivity. If they could get us to hand it over, free of charge, no doubt they would insist. But they can't get that, so maybe they can get it piecemeal. It would then be a question of: "We want what you have, so hand it over, bit by bit." That's covetousness. It's the basis of extortion. They want to keep the victims alive and working as slaves.

This is what strategic planners are counting on when they say, "The Soviets target weapons, not civilians."

Envy is different, however, and a lot more difficult to deal with. The Soviets see that the West is racing ahead of them economically, by every known measure. The Soviet leaders resent this. It testifies daily to the failure of Marxism. It is increasingly likely that the envy motive will take over. Even though they may lose lots of imported grain if they wipe us out, they may think that it's worth it. It's increasingly a question of: "We want everything you have. We probably can't get all of it. Better that nobody should have any of it. We'll destroy it . . . *all* of it."

The Ultimate Military Victory

There is one final—*really* final—consideration: they have a huge biological weapons research program to develop organisms that could kill the American people but leave our buildings and industry untouched.

As long as we have no civil defense shelters, we will remain open to this sort of attack, too.

The Guinness Book of World Records has a category for total number of people murdered in mass killings. By the Guinness estimates, the death camps of Hitler's Nazi Germany rate only a poor third place. Second place goes to the Soviets for the slaughter of their own citizens. First place goes to the Red Chinese during the years that they were under Soviet domination. First place in the category of percentage of an entire country killed goes to the Communists of Cambodia who murdered by bayonet and club over one-third of the Cambodian people between 1975 and 1979. The current Soviet slaughter of the people of Afghanistan may soon rival this Cambodian record.

During the time that the Soviets have been building their vast military advantage, they have taken great care to avoid a confrontation that might mobilize American public opinion. They have made the most astounding increase in military power in a 20-year period that the world has ever seen, but "the world" really hasn't seen it. Yet.

The question has to be: Will it pay them to destroy or neutralize the United States in one strike making it impossible for the rest of the world to do anything about it? They had a similar opportunity in 1969, when they could have hit the Red Chinese nuclear plants, and they missed it. Will they miss again?

Let us end with this observation. The United States military does not provide underground blast shelters for most of its own members. Not only do U.S. citizens have no civil defense, but the U.S. military is equally vulnerable. A first-strike nuclear attack against our ground-based military forces leave this nation without even ground troops to defend us.

At least the military is fair-minded in a perverse sort of way: if the U.S. public isn't going to be protected, neither are our soldiers.

After a nuclear strike against an unsheltered U.S. population, those Cuban troops would need little aid from any of the 215 Soviet divisions.

Conclusion

We have outlined the *minimal* statistics concerning the crisis. For those of you who want even more statistics, charts, and graphs, you can get a free copy of a sobering report, *Can America Catch Up?*

Committee on the Present Danger
905 Sixteenth St., N.W.
Washington, D.C. 20006

Another equally terrifying assessment is the study by Crommelin and Sullivan, *Soviet Military Supremacy.* It can be ordered for $5.95 from

Citizens Foundation
1701 Pennsylvania Avenue
Washington, D.C. 20006

The growth of Soviet power is relentless. The retreat of the West seems equally relentless. The nation is on auto-pilot, and our leaders are in the back of the plane, celebrating. It's party time. And the passengers are anesthetized.

This sleepwalking cannot go on forever. The Soviets are not building up this historically unprecedented arsenal for the fun of it.

Unless there is a miracle—a miracle based on something other than military production—we are going to see the tragic events played out in our day. We are in a sleepwalker's paradise. It cannot last.

If a nuclear world war were to begin today, the Communists would win. Such a war cannot now be won by the West militarily. In ten years, maybe, but not now. By giving the Pentagon more money, without imposing a wholly new strategy based on a passive civil defense system that will protect U.S. citizens, we are wasting time and money. We also need a new active defense system, with a new military strategy to go with it. *But we must begin with the protection of our population.* Without this, we are vulnerable to annihilation, while the Soviets are not. Without shelters, it will continue to be unilaterally assured destruction.

We need to warn the reader that the authors don't think that comparing military equipment is the most important thing in this analysis. We are warned against relying on "chariots."

Some trust in chariots, and some in horses, but we will remember the name of the Lord our God (Psalm 20:7).

The problem comes when two armies are facing each other, and the army of the nation that once relied on God now places faith in military hardware. *Then* the exercise of counting chariots becomes depressing for those who are still trying to remain faithful to God. They begin to count the enemy's chariots, as they did in the days of the prophet Isaiah, and they find: ". . . their land is also full of horses, neither is there any end of their chariots" (Isaiah 2:7). So it is today.

3

WHAT THEY HAVE
THAT WE DON'T

Most Americans assume that civil defense either takes care of itself somehow, or else that it's not really needed any more. Either that, or they think that a nuclear war will end the world. Neither assumption is true.

Let's consider the assumption that civil defense takes care of itself. This complacent attitude toward civil defense is somewhat reasonable, assuming you live in Red China, the Soviet Union, or Switzerland. In those nations, civil defense does take care of itself today . . . by systematically training the whole population to use the excellent shelter facilities already in place. Unquestionably, their people *have* been taken care of. The problem is, *we* haven't been.

Red China
We are about to describe the most remarkable low-technology, high-manpower civil defense system

in history. Only one word adequately describes it: *stupendous*.

The Red Chinese are deadly serious about the possibility of nuclear war. They should be. The Soviets almost launched a nuclear war against them in 1969.

H. R. Haldeman, who was President Nixon's chief of staff, wrote a book about his years in the Nixon administration. He reports that in 1969 the Soviets repeatedly approached the Nixon administration with a proposal: a joint nuclear first strike against Red China's atomic plants. When they were rebuffed by the U.S., they decided to do it on their own. If the U.S. government were simply to remain silent, the attack would take place.

The Nixon administration responded by resuming talks with the Chinese government after years of zero contact. This sent a message to the Soviet leaders, Haldeman argues. "The Soviets were on the brink of war. They believed that if the Chinese nuclear plants were destroyed, China would not be a military threat to them for decades. They teetered on the edge for days watching the Chinese moving more and more under the U.S. security umbrella. Finally, the Soviets realized that they no longer could take the chance. Intelligence photos showed their nuclear armed divisions were withdrawing from the Chinese border."[1]

Haldeman's account has received confirmation

---

1. H. R. Haldeman, *The Ends of Power* (New York: Times Books, 1978), p.93.

from Arkady Shevchenko. Mr. Shevchenko is the highest-ranking Soviet official ever to defect to the West. At the time he defected, he was Under Secretary General of the United Nations. In his book about his experiences as a Soviet official, he reveals that in 1969 Chinese border troops had briefly invaded the U.S.S.R. and had killed several Soviet soldiers. This outraged the Soviets, but it also frightened them. They feared a major invasion. They are paranoid about a billion Chinese on their border.

"From others I heard that the Soviet leadership had come close to using nuclear arms on China." The Defense Minister, Marshal Andrei Grenchko, had proposed using a huge hydrogen bomb against them, one which might produce fallout all over the Far East.[2] This was precisely the weapon that Haldeman says the U.S. believed they would use, and U.S. authorities feared massive fallout problems.

Shevchenko says that Soviet middle-level foreign affairs bureaucrats began to inquire about the U.S. reaction. Ambassador Dobrynin reported that the U.S. might react negatively and that U.S.-Soviet relations would be damaged. The leaders decided against the attack, but placed nuclear weapons and troops along the disputed border. Haldeman also noted this. Soviet relations with China got worse.

---

2. Arkady Shevchenko, *Breaking With Moscow* (New York: Knopf, 1985), p. 165.

The Chinese recognized the Soviet threat. They began to build tunnels under their major cities, tunnels the likes of which no one had ever seen before. They put the people to work in their leisure hours, so-called. Here is a report from political scientist Ishwar Ojha of Boston University, who visited Peking:

> One morning, in Peking, they told us they wanted to show us some tunnels. Now who wants to see tunnels when you are in Peking? We said, "Well, wouldn't it be nice if we could go out to the countryside and see a commune?" And they said, "No, no, you really must see these tunnels." So they took us to the busiest marketing section of Peking and into a large department store. And on the counter they pressed a button: the counter rolled away, and we saw steps leading down. We went down about eight meters, about 28 feet, and found tunnels, all right — well-built brick and concrete tunnels, miles and miles of them. The entire city of Peking, they told us, has tunnels under it, with an entrance from every department store, every apartment building, every residence. Inside the tunnels we saw kitchens, running water, sanitary facilities, food storage, medical facilities, all ready for use. In the event of a nuclear attack, they said, Peking's 7 million people can be safe in the tunnels in seven minutes, and can walk through them to 20

miles outside the city. And they told us that, since 1968, every major city in China has had similar tunnels built. So whenever we went to another city, we asked to see the tunnels — and they were there.[3]

In their introduction to a translation of a Chinese civil defense manual, two of America's foremost experts in civil defense comment on this effort.

> The unprecedented civil defense effort of the People's Republic of China, carried out by the masses during the 1970's, has aroused the interest and curiosity of all men concerned with the strategies and prevention of nuclear war. American visitors to the new China, including high officials and noted correspondents, have walked through miles of the thousands of miles of inter-connected tunnel-shelters that Chinese citizens have built under all their larger cities. . . . According to some American and Chinese observers, China has expended more person-hours of labor and more materials to build tunnels under her cities than were used to build the Great Wall.[4]

---

3. *Protect & Survive Monthly & British Civil Defence News* (July 1981), pp. 32-33.

4. Conrad V. Chester and Cresson H. Kearny, "U.S. Editors' Foreword," *Chinese Civil Defense*, excerpts translated from *Basic Military Knowledge*, a set of Books for the Self-Instruction of Young People (Shanghai, 1975) (Springfield, Virginia: National Technical Information Service, 1977), p. ix.

Additionally, some of their factories and other production facilities are underground. There is little doubt that these reports describe *the most effective urban civil defense system on earth*. The ability of the Chinese to move their urban residents to safety within ten minutes and then remove them entirely from the danger zone is unprecedented.

This invulnerability to nuclear annihilation by the Soviet Union may be as good a reason as any for the Soviets' unwillingness so far to use their missiles against either the U.S. or Red China. An unsuccessful nuclear attack against China would deplete their missile supply, and they would then have a dragon by the tail. They would be facing a billion outraged Chinese who would never forget. The Soviets know that they are facing a crisis on their border; it can only get worse.

On the other hand, a launch against the United States may soon be worth the risk, especially since the Soviets are now getting an anti-missile defense system in place. We are limited in what we could do to retaliate today; within a short time — perhaps even by the time this book has reached you — we will be virtually defenseless.

Soviet Union

The Soviets are very serious about protecting their people from a nuclear attack. The Soviets have spent the equivalent of about a hundred billion dollars on their civil defense shelters.[5] They also con-

5. Quentin Crommelin, Jr. and David S. Sullivan, *Soviet Military Supremacy* (Washington, D.C.: Citizen's Foundation, 1985), p. 52. This book was a project of the Defense and Strategic Studies Program, University of Southern California.

tinue to spend from $8 to $20 per person per year to maintain these shelters, improve civil defense training, and add more facilities. This compares with about 50 cents a year that the U.S. government spends on civil defense per citizen, and almost all of this is spent on salaries of the civil defense bureaucracy.[6] When the sirens sound, their salaries won't offer the public any shelter.

In the Soviet Union, about 100,000 full-time civilian and military personnel are involved in civil defense during peacetime, plus up to 20 million part-time personnel.[7] The Young Pioneers youth group trains children in civil defense. School children receive 15 hours of training per year. Adults get 20 hours. In technical institutes with two-year programs, 35 hours must be devoted to civil defense instruction.[8] The United States had a much less extensive but valuable civil defense training program in the 1960s which has now been completely abandoned.

Civilian Protection

During the 1960s the Soviets developed a civil defense plan based on evacuation. This has been gradually replaced by an in-place blast shelter system. Today, according to studies by E.N. York of Boeing

---

6. Cresson H. Kearny, *Nuclear War Survival Skills* (Oak Ridge, Tennessee: Oak Ridge National Laboratory, 1980), p. 5.

7. Leon Goure, "Civil Defense & Nuclear War," *Protect & Survive Monthly* (July 1981) p. 29. Dr. Goure is recognized as one of America's experts in Soviet civil defense.

8. Bruce Sibley, "The Strategic Significance of Soviet Civil Defense," *Protect & Survive Monthly* (August 1981), p. 23.

Company, about 75% of their people (the other 25% are in remote locations) are protected by blast shelters with an average of 62 psi sure-safe blast resistance. (This means that the shelters are 100% safe from a 62 pound per square inch blast wave. This includes most of the air-burst nuclear threat.) Moreover, hundreds of thousands of Soviets in the "Nomenklatura" (the ruling class) have now been given 1000 psi blast protection which makes them immune to most ground bursts as well.

By comparison, a 5 psi blast wave will reduce a frame building to rubble. The blast shelters which we propose in this book for the American people have a sure-safe blast resistance of about 200 psi.

The Soviets have constructed a system that will protect most of them. They have a huge nation geographically, and unlike the United States, their populations are not concentrated on the seacoasts. They have adopted a multi-level program of shelters that we do *not* recommend. They have divided their people into several groups. The closer to a city you are and the higher your personal position in Soviet society, the more expensive and blast-resistant your shelter. (We recommend equal, high-quality protection for every U.S. resident.) The Soviets have provided shelter space for virtually everyone in the country.

Our strategic planners after 1961 bet the survival of the United States on the doctrine that neither side would ever launch a first strike because the opponent could annihilate the first nation's citizens in a retaliatory attack. This defenseless position is no longer true of the Soviet population. It is still true of the U.S. population.

Industrial Protection

The Soviets have also built their industrial base as any sensible military dictatorship would. It is dispersed across a large land mass, and a considerable part of it is either underground or protected. Something in the range of 60 percent of new Soviet industrial plant construction since 1966 has been dispersed away from towns and cities.[9]

Here is what a mid-1970s Boeing Company study concluded: in the event of a USSR-US nuclear war, only 25 percent to 50 percent of the targeted industrial capacity of the Soviet Union would be destroyed in the primary target areas. Supporting industries would do even better: 75 percent of their blast furnaces, 75 percent of their foundries, 90 percent of their machine shops, 80 percent of their steel-fabricating facilities, and 80 percent of their aircraft manufacturing would survive. They could compensate for most of the damage by increasing their labor schedule from two shifts to three shifts a day.[10]

In short, our missiles cannot kill many of their people or destroy their industry. That is not true, unfortunately, of a first strike by them against us.

Switzerland

Everyone knows about Switzerland: the Alps, ski resorts, secret bank accounts, fine watches, choco-

---

9. *Ibid.*, p. 21.

10. Peter C. Hughes and M. R. Edwards, "Nuclear War in Soviet Military Thinking — The Implications for U.S. Security," *Journal of Social and Political Affairs* (April 1976), p. 124.

late, neutrality, eight centuries of local democratic rule, peace and prosperity. They haven't had to fight a war in five centuries. This is remarkable for a nation no larger than two New Jerseys, located in the middle of endlessly war-torn Europe.

What isn't generally known outside of Switzerland is that the entire Swiss population is now sheltered from atomic attack. Specialists may debate just how well they are sheltered, but specialists enjoy debating. They can safely ignore the United States because there is no debate over our shelters: there aren't any.

The Swiss have about 625,000 men in their armed forces, a little under ten percent of the Swiss population. This is the equivalent of an American army of 23 million. Our entire armed forces total a little over two million, of whom about half a million are stationed outside the United States.[11]

Theirs is a civilian army. Every able-bodied adult male serves for at least three decades. First, he serves full time for training and then in the reserve. At retirement at age fifty, he then serves another decade in the civil defense program. (People who are draft-deferred serve from age 20 to 60 in the civil defense program.)[12] Younger men ages 20-32 serve for three weeks a year. It drops to two weeks every two years for ages 33-42, and then falls to two one-

---

11. *Statistical Abstract of the United States*, 1985 (Washington: Government Printing Office, 1984), pp. 8, 340.

12. John Christiansen and Reed H. Blake, "Shelters and Service: The Twin Pillars of Switzerland's Civil Defense," *Journal of Civil Defense* (June 1985), p. 19.

week tours, ages 43-50. Each man takes his army-issue assault rifle (an automatic or machine gun) and his ammunition home with him and keeps it there. They are a peaceful, prosperous, freedom-loving, low-crime, heavily armed camp.

Swiss bridges are mined, the army has military bunkers all over the country, and there are high-technology defense installations. The Swiss could be defeated by the Soviet Union, but *they could not be defeated before they inflicted very high losses on the invaders.* They impose a high risk-reward ratio on invaders. That fact kept Hitler out of Switzerland. It is a fact of survival for the Swiss. The gains of conquest compared to the probable costs have not been sufficiently great in any potential invader's eyes since the day five centuries ago that the Swiss decided to become rigorously neutral. They have paid the price of preparedness in order to make any invader pay a much higher price.

A Swiss officer says, "In the Second World War, the will to defend was absolutely there. That will is very much unbroken."[13] The will to defend: this is the key. This is a sign of *the will to resist.* This will to resist is essential to the preservation of Western civilization against the forces of despotism and tyranny. These forces have always existed, but today these totalitarian forces are the best-armed in man's history.

The Swiss for 30 years have required home builders to install basement blast shelters in all new

---

13. Cited by John McPhee, *La Place de la Concorde Suisse* (New York: Farrar/Straus/Giroux, 1984), p. 26. This book is in English, but it has a French title.

homes. The Swiss government pays part of the cost of these shelters. Civil defense construction is a major industry in the private sector of the economy.[14]

The Swiss have spent the equivalent of $1,000 per person to build underground shelters for the Swiss population. These shelters are much more spacious (and five times as expensive per person) than the design we recommend. While we would like to see Swiss-type shelter living conditions in all U.S. shelters, we are aware of political realities. Voters are unlikely to succeed in pressuring the U.S. government to spend $250 billion on shelters.

So we face that other kind of pressure: 200 pounds per square inch.

Conclusion

About 28 percent of the world's civilian population is completely protected. The two Communist superpowers have understood the realities of nuclear war and international power politics. So have the Swiss. There are substantial civil defense programs in some other countries such as Sweden. The rest of the world, especially the U.S., has not understood.

There is a reason why the Communist powers are prepared for nuclear war: they plan on fighting one. They are both prepared to take the steps necessary to provide themselves with not only a fighting chance, but also a high probability of victory.

---

14. John Christiansen and Reed H. Blake, "Shelters and Service; The Twin Pillars of Switzerland's Civil Defense," *Journal of Civil Defense* (June 1985), p. 18.

The West is no longer a major military problem for China or the Soviet Union. They are major problems for each other. The best evidence of the West's impotence is its refusal to build civil defense shelters for its citizens. Whatever games the West may be playing, the game of serious international power politics is not one of them.

If our enemies are at some point willing to bring the "game" to its climax, 200 million Americans will die, unless we develop *and deploy* new defensive strategies. Some of these are active defense strategies, such as the strategic defense initiative (S.D.I.), also called Star Wars. They may or may not be built. The experts keep arguing about the details. Critics complain that a space-based defense wouldn't be perfect. It would, however, be good enough to preserve our nation, protect most of our property, and probably deter an attack if it is used in combination with a good civil defense system. Being continually at the mercy of the Soviet General Staff isn't so terrific, either. With a civil defense system (yes, it's also imperfect), other active defense systems would greatly strengthen the ability of the U.S. population to survive an atomic attack.

Today, we have no shelters. We have no anti-missile and anti-aircraft defense. We are at the mercy of the Soviet General Staff. We have very little ability to retaliate with nuclear weapons.

What should be argued no longer is the need for a place for our people to hide when the missiles begin to fly. Today, there is no way for the United States' military to shoot down the missiles before they reach their targets. Those of us who are targets — and this may mean all of us — want to get out of range. There is only one way to get out of range: *to dig.* The first step is to build a passive defense system.

What we recommend is simple: *the power of positive digging.*

Part II
TECHNICAL SOLUTIONS

4

SUBWAY TO SURVIVAL

Hiroshima and Nagasaki. These two Japanese cities are famous. Nuclear war began there in August of 1945.

The stories of the post-attack horrors are legendary. Some of the horrors were just that: legends. Stories about horrible deaths from *residual* radiation and legions of deformed children have no basis in fact. They are just false stories.

Over 100,000 people were killed in the combined raids. Another 200,000 were injured. The combined population of the two cities before the attacks had been 450,000 people. But these statistics don't tell the most important aspect of the story. There was a major reason for the high casualty rates: *the people were not inside bomb shelters*.

At Hiroshima, the air raid warning at 7 A.M. was lifted at 8 A.M. A mildly worded radio warning was issued at 8 A.M. telling people that they didn't have to go into the shelters unless B-29 bombers were spotted. The three B-29s appeared, but they were thought to be conducting a reconnaissance mission, not a bombing raid. At 8:15 the bomb exploded. It blew away a big chunk of Hiroshima. It also blew away the post-war hope of peacetime security.

Three days later in Nagasaki, an air raid warning was sounded at 11 A.M. Two minutes later the bomb exploded. Many people ignored the warning (there had been an earlier one which had been cancelled at 8:30). Some people actually stood and watched the two planes high in the sky. The bomb exploded two minutes after 11. (They obviously hadn't been told by their government what had happened to Hiroshima. Bureaucrats hate to report bad news, even when your life depends on it.)

One woman was standing inside an earthen bomb shelter. She was about 300 feet from the entrance, which had no door or other blast-resistant barrier at the other end. The bomb exploded about 500 yards up and 200 yards horizontally from the shelter's entry way, or about the length of two football fields. The blast knocked her down, and she was burned on the back of her legs and on the upper part of her right arm. She was later interviewed about her experiences. No burns were inflicted on any part of her body that had been covered by clothing. Another woman, who had been closer to the entrance, was burned, but she recovered with no after-effects.

Around the corner from the first woman, about 12 feet away, were several other people. They were uninjured by the explosion. That corner of earth had been sufficient protection.

These were not sophisticated shelters designed to

withstand anything like an atomic explosion. They were simple earthen tunnels. The problem was that most of them were empty when the bombs went off, except for workers who were inside repairing them.

"Big" Bombs

The Hiroshima and Nagasaki bombs were "small" atomic bombs, 12 kilotons and 20 kilotons. (A "kilo" means 1,000.) Today's common nuclear bombs are anywhere from ten to fifty times more powerful than the two Hiroshima and Nagasaki bombs in terms of the equivalent number of tons of TNT, but because of the laws of physics, the bomb's effects diminish rapidly the farther away you are from the detonation. A one-megaton bomb is fifty times more powerful than the Nagasaki bomb at the point of detonation, but its effects are not fifty times more powerful a block away, or a mile away, or three miles away. In fact, the farther away you are from the point of detonation, the less the measurable difference in intensity.

This is why both the U.S. and the U.S.S.R. have quit deploying the older huge bombs of the early 1960s and have instead adopted a strategy of deploying many more smaller bombs. It is far more devastating to a city to be hit by ten well-targeted half-megaton bombs than by a single five-megaton bomb, and modern technology now permits very accurate placement of the bombs.

As an example of this effect of "less devastation at a distance," the people who survived in a tunnel 200 yards from ground zero would probably have survived a bomb ten times as large had they been 500 yards from the explosion, and would have survived the largest bomb currently deployed by the Soviets at 1,000 yards distance.

Remember also that the Nagasaki bomb shelter had no blast door, and was above ground in the side of a dirt hill, so the blast blew straight down that tunnel. What if the shelter had had a blast door? Would the woman even have been knocked down and burned? Definitely not—not even if the blast had been directly overhead.

"Subways" Are for Surviving

Let's imagine a situation that we all hope will never take place. You hear air raid sirens, and you turn on your radio or television. You're told to turn to a special frequency for emergency instructions. You do this, and you hear that an attack is imminent.

Question: Would you save your life and your family's lives, if you could survive in a New York City subway car? Or would you sit there, waiting for nuclear disaster, because you just couldn't face the thought of spending a few days in a subway car?

The answer is obvious. A week or two in a subway car is preferable to being incinerated, or killed when your house falls on top of you, or death by subsequent nuclear fallout. Two weeks in a crowded New York subway car is not anyone's idea of fun, but it sure beats dying in an atomic attack.

Here is the amazing fact: it is possible to save most of the U.S. population from perishing during an atomic attack, at least under most circumstances, by constructing underground shelters that would involve the same degree of crowding as a New York subway car's legal capacity. We are not talking about rush-hour crowding, but simply the maximum capacity for which the car was specifically designed.

If nobody goes into the shelters, it won't work, just as shelters didn't work at Hiroshima and Nagasaki. If the officials in charge refuse to issue an alert, not many citizens will survive a nuclear attack. But that's the case today even if officials did issue an alert. Hardly anyone would survive. We have no "subway cars" to get into. It makes sense to issue an alert if there is something people can do to protect themselves. It doesn't make much sense to scare everyone into a panic by issuing an alert if there isn't anything that the nation's people can do to protect themselves. And today, there isn't anything effective we could do.

Civil defense scientists have developed some expedient procedures for protection after evacuation, but these require very long warnings before an attack, 24 to 48 hours.

The Soviet Union has a sufficient number of deliverable nuclear weapons to destroy every city and large town in the U.S. There are very few people in the United States who are not living today in or near a targetable town or city. Moreover, fallout is a threat to most of our rural population; so is the danger from the blast of bombs that miss their urban or military targets.

If an attack comes without warning, then fewer

people will survive. But more people could survive a surprise attack than if there were no shelters at all. In any case, it is likely that there will be at least some tell-tale signs of an imminent attack. But if we don't get some protection, then all the tell-tale signs in the world won't do us much good. A few thousand senior political officials and military leaders may get their families to greater safety, but the rest of us will suffer the consequences of having no hole in the ground to crawl into.

Under present circumstances, only those people who live in the countryside or in very small towns that are not downwind from nuclear fallout are protected today. They are protected by default: they aren't worth a bomb.

A Ticket to Survival

We are proposing the mass production of highly resistant shelters that are not much more comfortable than a subway car. The goal is *survival, not comfort*. We need the equivalent of boot camp, not a vacation in Hawaii. We can't afford luxurious shelters; if we are willing to accept this reality, then we *can* afford top-quality construction that will protect virtually everyone who is inside. (Actually, we can afford better shelters than any country on earth, but the government refuses to spend the money to protect us. We voters have not made our greatest concern—survival—clear to them in the only way our elected federal officials understand: "Vote for a shelter system, or we will elect a Congress that will!" If they believe we will do this, they will get the shelters built.)

What kind of protection do we need? There are five things that can kill people during an atomic attack:

Initial nuclear radiation (duration: about one second)
Heat (duration: a few seconds)
Blast (duration: a few seconds)
Burial or bombardment by flying or falling objects
Fallout

The first two killers get you first. If you survive the first two, the blast comes roaring toward you at about the speed of sound (about 700 miles an hour). It is accompanied by a wind that blows at the equivalent of 1,000 miles an hour, if you're very close; less, if you're farther away. In a few seconds this passes, leaving behind rubble where there had been buildings and homes. It literally knocks over homes like a giant bulldozer.

The fourth killer is a secondary effect. Bricks, pieces of glass, and other objects become lethal if they're flying by at hundreds of miles an hour. Being inside a room with a window during a nuclear explosion can be fatal, even if the room doesn't collapse on you, which it will if you are within a few miles of the explosion. (Naturally, it all depends on such factors as distance, what's in between your building and the explosion, the size of the bomb, and so forth. Scientists who happen to be on a small farm in the country the day we are attacked will be able to argue with each other over what really killed you, if there's anything left behind to argue about. You get the general idea: nuclear explosions can kill people.)

Fifth, there can sometimes be a post-attack killer: fallout—but only if a nuclear bomb has exploded at ground level. (Nobody was killed by fallout radiation in Hiroshima and Nagasaki, because the bombs were detonated in the air.) When a bomb is detonated on the ground, it pulls up dirt and dust into the famous mushroom cloud, where it then becomes radioactive. Beginning about a half hour later, this now-radioactive dirt drifts down, especially downwind. If it gets on you, and you don't wash it off immediately, or if you can't hide under a barrier, for example, of six feet of concrete or ten feet of earth, it will kill you. You can stand some exposure to it, but you must seek shelter soon. (See Appendix 5 for a more complete description of fallout.)

This fallout is dangerous briefly. It "wears out" rapidly—usually within a week or two. It is dangerous because it has a rapid rate of decay. Things that decay slowly aren't dangerous, but things that decay rapidly aren't dangerous for very long. The secret is to get away from it for a few days—perhaps up to two weeks. "Away from it" means, for example, behind (or under) a barrier of several feet of dirt or concrete.

Protection from radiation is very simple and effective with shelter. Without shelter, more than half of those killed by the attack would die from initial nuclear radiation (duration: one second) and the subsequent fallout. This would involve great suffering over several days or weeks, since radiation sickness is a prolonged, terrible illness. Burn and burial victims would also die slowly and in horrible agony.

What if we could get into a shelter that would protect us from all five possibilities? What if we could survive anything except a direct explosion at ground level immediately above our heads? (There won't be many of these explosions because they don't do enough damage to the buildings: less bang for the buck, less rubble for the ruble.)

If we can show you that you could survive all five, would you buy a lifetime ticket on the "subway" for $300? Would you buy tickets for your family members? If you could charge it to your credit card today, would you do it?

If you don't have the cash right·now, would you be willing to ask your Congressman to buy one for you and bill it to your credit card, with payment due next April 15? We know *we* would be willing.

And if your Congressman says we can't afford it, that America has too much debt as it is, perhaps you could suggest something else that he might cut out of the budget to make room for your family's survival. We think there must be something less important than that on the list.

What do we need to survive a nuclear attack? Not many citizens know. Let's take a look at the "subway" and find out.

The Accommodations

The shelter system which we suggest allocates $200 per sheltered space to the shelter itself, plus

$100 per person to post-attack food, survival, and re-building supplies. This is the minimum for assured survival. An additional $50 per person would mark-edly improve the comfort of shelter occupants by providing each one with more space.

To keep costs down to a bare minimum, the shel-ters will be crowded. They will not be crowded to the point of endangering anyone's life, just to the point of guaranteeing everyone's increasing discomfort. We assume that adults who get too uncomfortable after a few days inside will be given the option of going outside the shelter before the fallout has become safe. We think that most people will prefer crowded conditions to wide-open radioactive spaces. But they should be given a choice.

In those areas where there is no fallout, everyone can leave the shelters after the attack is over. If ground bursts and wind conditions result in fallout, then people will need protection from the fallout for a few days or weeks. In many places, this protection will be available outside the shelters. Where it isn't, a stay in the shelters for as much as two weeks could be necessary. As fallout radiation diminishes, people could go outside for increasing periods of time each day.

Meanwhile, they will be packed in like . . . well, like New Yorkers. Each shelter will hold about 150 people. (See Appendix 3 for details.) Given the size of each shelter, this means that each person will oc-cupy about 2.3 square feet of floor space and 21 cubic feet. This is the same space as that required in Ger-man bunkers during World War II. (Those famous

German bunkers were actually above ground: several stories of thick concrete structures disguised so that pilots would think they were normal buildings. Despite all the bombing and the firestorms, people who were inside them survived.)

This space is about one-half the standard for Soviet and Swedish shelters, and is about *one-half the space per person in economy class on a 747 airplane.* The cost of increasing the available space to the Soviet standard of 5 square feet per person would be an additional $50 per person. This would be a desirable additional expenditure.

To achieve maximum occupancy, some people will be sleeping in hammocks that hang from the ceiling. Others will be sitting down. Everyone else will be standing. People will then take turns in each assignment.

There will be two small, limited bathroom chambers.

To keep out the blast, and also to guard against any use of chemical or biological weapons, the shelters can be sealed up tightly. Each shelter will contain bottled oxygen. Cylinders that contain compressed oxygen and trays of material that absorb exhaled carbon dioxide cost about $12 per person per day. We recommend a minimum of two days' worth of air per person per shelter. Then the shelters can be "buttoned up" for maximum safety.

The shelters will also be equipped with filtered ventilation systems that bring in outside air. Filters will keep out radioactive materials, biological organisms, and poison gas. The ventilation system also carries away heat and keeps the shelters at a comfortable temperature. If the shelters need to be "buttoned up," then the secondary water-cooling system takes over. The shelter is built over a well for this purpose.

Building a shelter over a water well is fairly simple in most regions of the country. All Soviet shelters, like the German WWII bunkers, are required to include a well. The water can be pumped through cooling pipes to reduce internal heat. This is a more effective approach than to rely exclusively on air ventilation. Heat must be dissipated.

Each shelter will have drinking water and food. Food isn't absolutely crucial, contrary to overfed popular opinion. Most of us could survive for several weeks without food, but for basic satisfaction, we need to eat. Water, however, is vital.

A basic medical kit will be in every shelter. So will radios and radiation meters that have been shielded inside the shelter from what scientists call the electromagnetic pulse (EMP). EMP is a nuclear weapons effect that blows out electrical circuits that are attached to power lines, antennae, and unshielded circuit wires.

Each of the shelters will have to contain some books on rebuilding after an attack, some instructions on measuring radiation, and similar survival information. The shelters will have other tools, including shovels, cutting torches, and fire extinguishers.

In Appendix 3, we include a more complete list of shelter contents. The shelters are survival-oriented, not underground equivalents of the Holiday Inn. Staying in one for two weeks will be an experience you will never forget, and you won't want to remember. Compared to dying, they are marvelous.

Ask the Red Chinese, the Russians, and the Swiss. They already have protection. We don't.

But our leaders in their wisdom did install some air raid sirens. Maybe they still work.

Conclusion

The "subway" system isn't the only way to gain the protection we need. There are others. This system can be built quickly and effectively *now* at low cost. Research on shelters has been going on at laboratories around the country for over 30 years. That research shows that this system would unquestionably work.

It has one major technical drawback: it won't work if it isn't built.

5

SCHOOLS FIRST

You want your kids to have a fighting chance. Agreed? Even if it costs you an extra few hundred dollars over the next year, that's what you want. You can get it, *if you can convince Congress*.

Believe it or not, you can get it before the next school term starts. All it takes is a decision by Congress and the support of the President.

If your house were on fire, you'd grab your kids and run for an exit. But what if the doors were locked every night by Congressional order? What if some bureaucrat made it impossible for you to get out of your house, even though the whole world knows that there is a team of professional arsonists loose in the neighborhood?

Well, there is such a team. It's called the Soviet Union. And our political representatives have made it impossible for us to get out of the burning house. *They won't build us shelters*. They won't even build shelters for our children. Why not?

That's all we're asking the government to do initially: *build shelters at every school in the nation*, public and private, without discrimination of race, color, or creed. All the kids should be given a fighting chance to survive.

If the sirens go off, ten minutes later all of our kids could be safe in their shelters. If it happened during school hours, even a first strike by the Soviet Union aimed at our cities couldn't kill our kids. We would have at least 15 minutes' warning under the worst-case scenario. In 15 minutes, the entire school-age population in the U.S. could survive the blast and fallout. They could run for cover.

They could have serious bomb drills, the same way they have fire drills. (An un-serious bomb drill is one along the lines of "Get under your desks, children, since in fifteen minutes the school will be flattened." We both remember these from the 1950s. Maybe you do, too. In the 1950s, the Soviets didn't have 10,000 nuclear warheads for blanketing every city and most rural areas in the U.S. Schools *should* teach children about expedient responses such as dropping into a protected position away from windows if they sense a bomb flash without warning. There is however no technical substitute for shelters. None.)

If someone objects because bomb drills would be too scary for young children, would he also recommend that we stop having fire drills? What kind of nonsense is this? Fire drills aren't "doom and gloom" exercises. They're exercises that tell the kids there's safety available, that they aren't going to be killed in a fire. That's what bomb drills are, too. They are "move fast and survive" drills.

It *is* "doom and gloom" to allow our children to be held as captives by Soviet generals with their ability to incinerate our children. They can do that now. Unless we get shelters built this year, they will be able to do it next year, too.

Now, why won't Congress do something? Are they too cheap? Do our elected representatives really believe that voters are so cheap that they won't give their children a fighting chance?

If we really *are* that cheap, then we don't deserve to survive . . . and we probably won't.

Saving Our Kids

There are about 55 million children in school today in the U.S., from kindergarten through college. Because they are concentrated in small areas, they could get to shelters in a matter of minutes. Right there, you're talking about saving about a quarter of the U.S. population.

There are about 27 million children in elementary schools. They attend about 73,000 schools. That works out to about 370 children in each school. This means we would need to build only about two shelters per elementary school.

There are about 17 million high school children who attend about 30,000 schools. This averages to under 570 students per school. This means that we will need about four shelters per secondary school. Obviously, in urban areas, schools have more children. If an average urban school is 1,500 students, then ten shelters would protect them.

Teachers would have priority positions in the

shelters. When the sirens sound, they would be the adults who accompany the children. The children need adults to help them; school teachers are the ones available immediately.

Where would we put these shelters? Simple: under the playground in elementary schools and under the football and baseball fields at high schools. Installation would take two weeks in a crash program, a month at a normal construction rate. Shelters could be put under the baseball field during football season, and under the football field during baseball season.

Go team go! Nobody misses a game. And almost all of our kids survive a nuclear attack, even if it is aimed at civilians. They all survive fallout in a nuclear attack aimed at military targets.

But Congress says we have more important things to do with tax money.

Name three. Name one. Put a picture of your kids or grandkids in front of you, and then tell us what government spending program is worth risking their lives another year. Tell us what boondoggle is worth allowing the Soviet generals to use our children as hostages to their nuclear missiles another year. Or another month.

Dear Mr. Congressman

Suggestion: if you can't think of a spending program that is more important than the kids, tell your Congressman that if he keeps delaying and explaining and mumbling, you are going to vote for any opponent who guarantees that our kids' safety goes to the top of the list. You remind him that there is an election coming, and that you want some straight answers. Sample letter:

Dear Congressman:

I am tired of having my children held captive by Soviet generals who can press a few buttons and kill 50 million American kids 30 minutes later.

Do you intend to vote to install shelters for my children or grandchildren? Their names are: (   ). I want them protected. If you are not willing to have them protected, please tell me why. If you want them protected, then please support legislation now to get them protected immediately. I want a straight answer.

Just let me know by return mail how you intend to vote on installing shelters for the kids: thumbs up or thumbs down. Yes or no. It's a simple question, and it requires only a simple answer. An evasive answer means that you're against the idea. The kids can't be protected by an evasive answer.

Sincerely yours,

Your Name

That's the way you can get your kids protected. *That's the only way.* If you won't write this letter, or send a telegram, and *tell him you want action, and you want it now,* your kids won't get their shelters.

Congress thinks all those other programs are more important. If you won't tell your Congressman and two Senators what you really want, your children will remain hostages to the Soviet generals. The addresses are easy:

Congressman So and So
House Office Building
Washington, D.C. 20515

Senator Such and Such
Senate Office Building
Washington, D.C. 20510

All Congress has to do is appropriate the money. Congress should also offer incentives. For example, Congress could offer a grand prize of ten million dollars, plus $1,000 per shelter, to the first county in the country with over 25,000 kids enrolled in school that completes installation of a shelter for every enrolled student, public and private. Congress can also offer runner-up prizes: $5,000,000 (plus $500 per shelter) to the second one to finish, $1,000,000 (plus $250 per shelter) to the third, and $500,000 (plus $100 per shelter) to the fourth, and so on. We all hustle harder if there's a potential pay-off at the end of the competition. So do local politicians. Get the counties to race for just a little extra money. Get the bureaucrats to sweat a little. Better that some bureaucrats should sweat a little than have our kids kept hostage any longer.

Counties that balk lose a shot at a pile of extra money.

Military Second

Not only are U.S. children undefended, the U.S. Army is equally undefended. The Navy is too, of course, but that's inescapable. There are no shelters for surface ships — yes, even our growing navy of 500 high-technology floating targets.

Consider also the military implications of 25 active Cuban divisions just 90 miles from our shore. Consider the back-up potential of up to 215 Soviet divisions.

How long will our surviving children remain free if the eight Cuban runways start being used for transporting paratroopers? Who will defend the survivors if our ground-based military gets wiped out in a first strike?

U.S. Army bases provide no shelters. The buildings are not being built underground. The troops are helpless. The Soviets could destroy everyone stationed at most of our bases with a small part of their arsenal. They could use submarine-launched missiles and other less accurate missiles, since they would simply be aiming at men and buildings.

How long would our army last? We would have *zero* divisions 30 minutes after the launch. That's the shape national defense is in today. There isn't any. It's a myth — a 300 billion-dollar-a-year Pentagon myth. The generals refuse to protect their own troops.

Are they unaware of the problem? How could they be? They know what a nuclear explosion does. It is clear that they aren't allowed to build shelters.

Maybe the civilian advisors to the President have told him not to scare the voters by admitting that someone needs shelters. Maybe the advisors are afraid to ruffle the Soviets' feathers. But whatever the reason, no general resigns in protest and goes to the press to tell the truth. No general decides to sacrifice his career to save the lives of his men and to save the country. That is why this battle to get shelters for our citizens is so hard. The men who are supposed to lead are afraid to lead. They want to "work from the inside." They want to "work with the system."

The fact is, "the system"—the advisors to every President since John F. Kennedy—has not been willing to protect our people. The men under the command of today's generals have placed their lives in the hands of senior officers who have been unwilling to place the nation's safety and their troops' safety above their personal career goals. This is hard language, but our men in uniform need hard shelters. Now.

There are some military men (retired before or soon after they speak up) who have tried to warn us. Men like Knight, Keegan, Graham, Singlaub, and Walt, like Patton and MacArthur before them, are trying to save this country. For example, General Keegan recently said: "The Soviet Union is now in a position to launch, win, and survive World War III —and with fewer casualties than it suffered in the last World War." Unfortunately, most of the bureaucrats and politicians are ignoring them.

If the shelters are built, it will be very difficult for

the Soviets to destroy our ground forces in a first strike. If our troops have no shelters, they are as good as dead. So are the chances of rebuilding a politically independent country. We need our troops. We pay $300 billion a year to be defended, yet our soldiers are denied the simplest sort of protection. *Our government is telling our military personnel loud and clear that they aren't worth $200 each.*

We had better send our government an equally loud and clear message. The first priority of the military budget must be the protection of our troops. Yes, even above military pension benefits.

Conclusion

The conclusion is obvious: install shelters at every school, kindergarten through college, in the nation. Vote for the program immediately, and have them installed before the next school term. This can be done. *Accept no excuses* from elected officials. Either our children get protection, or else officials who oppose shelters for our children find new jobs.

If you don't care enough to send a letter at least to your Congressman, then you are not worried about 10,000 Soviet nuclear warheads. You are not worried that the Soviet generals are using your children or grandchildren as hostages to nuclear destruction.

But you *do* care. You *are* going to sit down, *now*, and write that letter. Because your kids' (or grandkids') lives are literally on the line.

Maybe you don't know the name of your Congressman or U.S. Senators. Don't feel embarrassed;

most people don't know. It's fairly easy to find out. Call your local library and ask for the reference department. The person there can tell you.

Will you make one telephone call to the library in order to give your children a fighting chance?

And while you're at it, tell your elected official to start pressuring the Pentagon to spend money to shelter our troops. They need shelters, too. We don't want our children growing up under President Castro.

6

WALK FOR YOUR LIFE

If we build enough shelters to protect school-age Americans, we can save the lives of 25 percent of all Americans. That is a major accomplishment. But what about the other 75 percent? What about the adults? What about keeping alive the people who are needed to help those children grow to maturity?

What about *you*?

We want to do more than provide a generation of students for Communist invaders to capture. We've seen what they've done in the past. They are not nice people.

Furthermore, what about after school? What if the siren sounds at 5 in the evening or 5 in the morning? Who gets in the shelters then? And how fast?

Extra Shelters

If we're willing to pay for shelters at the schools, why wouldn't we buy enough shelters to protect people in the suburbs? If the kids are at school, how difficult would it be to protect housewives? Could we protect people who work in the local community? Can it be done?

The answer is clear: the Soviets have done it, the Red Chinese have done it, and the Swiss have done it. Of course it can be done.

Where should we put them? One obvious possibility is in every neighborhood park. It's city property. Nobody has to have his building torn down to make room for a shelter.

Then there are parking lots. America has a lot of parking lots. They may be privately owned, but the shelters are underground. People inside stores can make a run for the shelters.

What store owner is going to resist being favored by an extra degree of safety for himself and his customers? What shopping mall will resist? "We want all of you to know that you can shop in greater safety at the shopping mall three blocks away, because we wouldn't allow the government to install some shelters. But shop here anyway." Not the best advertising campaign in the world, we think.

There are parking lots at nursing homes, hospitals, and almost every public building in the country.

What businessman would protest having a shelter in the back lot for himself and his employees? Not many. If one objects, there will be a dozen who will welcome the opportunity. If military tensions increase, it will make hiring employees easier for businessmen who have a shelter close at hand . . . or foot.

Most shelters can be put on publicly owned property. There shouldn't be much need for requiring owners of private land to put up with a few weeks of digging. It may happen occasionally that a small plot of above-ground private property has to be purchased, but not that often.

If there is no other location available, the shelters can be installed right under the streets.

The necessary space is available.

We've all seen movies about an atomic attack. They always include the same scene. The roads always jam up with cars, everyone is bumper to bumper, and only those who are conveniently out of town survive.

This famous scene is not in our scenario. What we recommend is the placement of very strong shelters close enough to home so that people can walk to them. (Frankly, we both intend to run.) If an attack takes place, most of the people will walk a block or two and get into a shelter. If they're smart, they'll run. *But they won't drive.* They won't have to.

These shelters, without evacuation, make certain that we can reach them in time. This is especially important to our older citizens, to parents carrying infants or dragging small children, and others who are less mobile. It is essential to all of us in case of surprise attack.

The Suburbs

Let's consider a city with a population density of 1,500 people per square mile. This would require the installation of ten shelters per square mile. They should be dispersed, so that the Soviets can't destroy clusters of shelters with a single bomb—assuming they would attack the shelters, which would be foolish militarily. They would then fail to destroy strategic targets. They wouldn't get the maximum rubble for the ruble. They would shoot their wad of warheads on people — and, as we'll show, they still would succeed in killing only 10 percent of the entire U.S. population with a 100 percent shelter-targeted, ground-burst attack. Presently, they can kill most of America's population, civilian and military, with only a small fraction of their total inventory of nuclear warheads.

About 50 percent of the American people live and work in areas with population densities of 1,500 people per square mile or less. By putting in a maximum of ten shelters per square mile, this half of the population could be protected. *Half!* Yet there are critics who refuse even to consider civil defense. They would throw away 115 million lives because they think it's too expensive to construct shelters.

How does anyone with a conscience write off 115 million people in the name of "fiscal responsibility"?

An additional 30 percent live in areas where the density is from 1,500 to 6,000 per square mile. In these areas we need to increase the concentration of shelters to a maximum of 40 per square mile. This will probably require some shelters to be put together in clusters. These somewhat more densely clustered shelters are still too far apart to be practical targets.

Downtown

About 20 percent of the U.S. population lives in densities above 6,000 people per square mile. In the central cities, population densities are quite high during working hours. For these areas, clusters of shelters will be built. The civil defense system will have to provide additional special shelters for the commuters in these densely populated areas. They will need shelters at home in suburbia in case of an evening attack, and they will also need shelters downtown near work. Residents will go to their local neighborhood shelters. Commuters will have to go into large shelters underneath the buildings in which they work, or else they will have to walk farther to get to extra local shelters.

Remember, most of the industrial capacity of the country *isn't* inside the main population regions of the largest cities. Which do the Soviets fear the most? The paper-shufflers or the blue-collar producers of iron and steel?

True, there is greater risk for people who live in the more densely populated areas, but they know that anyway. They have accepted that risk.

And remember: once the shelters are installed, if the Soviets then sensibly target military bases, factories, and above-ground real estate instead of our people, almost everyone inside those shelters is going to survive, too. Even to hope to win the war, *the Soviets would have to let our people survive in the shelters*. They don't have enough weapons to attack the shelters and military and industrial targets. Those in the shelters are threatened only by the blast, not fallout. If they survive the initial blast, they will survive the attack. The fallout can't kill them, since they're inside the shelters.

The federal government should build a local shelter for everyone near his home. Businesses or a commuter tax could finance extra shelters in the central cities for non-residents. Or, if voters around the country are willing to shoulder the extra tax burden, they can buy extra shelters for the commuters in the central cities. They will be more expensive, however: deeper holes, larger facilities, and more disruptive to build. The streets of New York City and Chicago are already clogged.

People who work in the downtown section of the very large cities face higher risks. They are more vulnerable targets. The Soviets can kill more people with ground bursts. But we are talking about only 20 percent of the population, and with shelters most of them would survive too. The Soviets would have to use hundreds of warheads to destroy the shelters of a city like New York City or Washington, D.C. (See Appendix 2—Shelter locations.)

If shelters were dug deeper in urban areas, the chance of survival would increase. Obviously, a wholly passive defense system cannot be expected by itself to offer the protection that combination with a successful active defense system would provide: an anti-ballistic missile defense, in other words—the kind of systems that the Soviets have installed in their cities and close to their military targets. Let's face it, without shelters, we're *all* totally vulnerable targets. Commuters into the big cities will face far fewer risks after a shelter system is built than all of us face today without a shelter system. If the Soviets expect to win, they cannot use their weapons on an ineffective attack on the shelters. Therefore, even the central city commuters will survive. Today, any kind of attack will wipe out commuters, residents, and the wife and kids at home.

We advocate a shelter system that will vastly reduce the risk of death during an attack.

Can shelters save 90% of the population? Yes. Moreover, the shelters make such undesirable targets of the civilians that the shelters would probably save *all* of them and *possibly even prevent nuclear war itself*.

Will shelters save them? It depends on whether people run for the shelters when the sirens go off. If some people don't get into shelters, then at least they *could have* saved their lives. (Remember those Japanese spectators at Hiroshima who stared into the sky to see what the three B-29s would do.) The government will have done its duty. The government should make available to everyone the *possibility* of protection.

So far, our argument assumes that only the federal government will build and install the shelters. This may be too restrictive an assumption. If state and local governments respond to local pressures to build additional shelters, then they can decrease the crowding in the shelters or else provide more safety for those in central cities. The federal government owes us a minimum fighting chance. It's their job to defend us from the effects of war. But every little bit helps. Other levels of civil government can get into the act. If we can get more money from local governments, we increase our survival chances.

Individuals will probably start installing private shelters, once the government has placed its "seal of approval" on the idea that shelters are a good idea. Their neighbors will not object, since this will make more space available in the public shelters. Once the "stigma" of trying to keep your family alive is removed, more families will install their own shelters. Private shelters are much more expensive, so only the wealthier people will build them.

It is depressing to think that in today's climate of opinion, it is considered anti-social to install a shelter for your family. This hostility to shelters has been produced by the government's head-in-the-sand attitude about the Soviet nuclear threat.

It's time for the government to get its head out of the sand and to get shelters into the ground.

Conclusion

Would it be worth $300 per family member to you to get a 90 percent (or more) chance of survival in an all-out atomic attack, including the tools to rebuild?

More to the point, would it be worth $300 per family member to construct a shelter system that would probably keep the Soviets from launching an attack, because they know that afterward they will be facing over 200 million fighting mad Americans? Would it be worth $300 per person to get out from under the Soviet blackmail threat? We think it would.

Congress says it's more than you're willing to pay. Congress says you want the money to be spent on more important things.

Write to your elected representatives. Ask them what things they think are more important. Get their answers in writing. Save their computerized letters to you; take them with you when it's time to vote in the next election. Here is the type of letter you might receive:

Dear Mr. Jones:

I was happy to receive your letter. I always like to hear from the voters. I, too, am very interested in civil defense. This important topic is very important. It is important that we all think a lot more about important topics. So rest assured, I am always thinking. This is important.

Very truly yours,

J. David Waffle

"When in doubt, mumble!" But you didn't elect him to mumble. You elected him to represent you. *Don't forget his mumbling when it's time to mark the ballot.* It won't do you much good to remember his mumbling when the sirens go off, so remember it when you vote.

We can all debate about politics. We can try to get our people elected. Americans love to fight about which politician is the best one. But the day the sirens go off, the debating is over if there aren't any shelters. Let's get first things first. Let's leave the debating for subjects that can still be debated after the sirens sound.

7

THE YEAR AFTER

A lot of people who saw it believe that the ABC television movie, "The Day After," was a multi-million dollar propaganda device. If it was, it was a flop. The public opinion poll taken the day after indicated that neither the movie nor the insufferably boring panel discussion that followed the movie changed anyone's opinion.

We are continually being propagandized to keep us from building defenses. A recent example is the so called "nuclear winter phenomenon." Completely discredited by numerous science and engineering studies, the *myth* of nuclear winter is still spread by uninformed people and by people who want to keep America defenseless.

"The Day After" was accurate in one very important respect: there would be enormous casualty levels if the United States were attacked before it had a simple but effective shelter system.

There are people who think that nuclear war unthinkable. These people clearly are not military strategists, who have thought abo fully for four decades.

There are actually a few people who think that life without luxuries for a few years wouldn't be worth living. They have a low view of the meaning and importance of life. We are not directing our arguments to change their minds about the benefits of a civil defense program. We are arguing to convince other people — people who, in a fire in the middle of the night, will grab their children and run out of the house.

People who think that nuclear war is unthinkable, and who believe that the Soviet Union's leaders think so too, should not be the ones who make the decision about building shelters for the country. Unfortunately for us, those are precisely the people who have had the political power to make this decision for the last 30 years. That's why we have no shelters today.

To discuss "the year after," we need to talk about two separate scenarios: the year after an atomic attack if we have shelters, and the year after a surrender to the Soviet Union because we don't have shelters. The third alternative, the year after an atomic attack if we don't have shelters, isn't worth discussing, unless you live in the mountains and speak Spanish or Russian, or unless you are interested in a description of the horrible, prolonged, lingering suffering and death that would come to most unsheltered Americans.

I. Survival with Shelters

There is a very real possibility that the Soviet Union's strategists will eventually resort to the use of nuclear war. They are building up their arsenal to blackmail us, at the very least. But they may decide that blackmail is too risky. The pace of results might be too slow for them. They may choose to make an example of us. Like the bully who beats up the strongest opponent in town, and then asks "Who's next?" so the Soviets, if they destroy the United States, might get the cooperation of every other victim—even the Chinese . . . for a while.

A. The Likelihood of an Attack

If we are protected from massive casualties in a first strike, we will be less likely to be attacked. The Soviets can be sure that we do not plan a first strike against them. We have a no first-strike policy. We don't have a sufficient number of weapons. Their factories are protected. Their people are protected. Ours aren't.

In some scenarios, an attack would be preceded by warnings. Today we probably would not be warned. There would be a news black-out. The nation's leaders would probably evacuate their families, but it would do no good to warn the rest of us. We have no shelters to go to.

(Yes, there are underground shelters for our nation's senior officials. They are scattered about an hour outside Washington, D.C. An article identifying a number of them was published in the now-defunct magazine, *Inquiry*, Feb. 2, 1981. But as the author says, a full-scale nuclear attack on Washington by submarine-launched missiles would take only 12 minutes to complete, so these shelters would useful only if there were considerable wa

Besides, they are no doubt targeted by the larger Soviet ICBMs.)

B. Rebuilding

Suppose, however, that we are still attacked after we build a civil defense system. Suppose that the attack is the worst nuclear attack possible with the Soviet arsenal. If we have saved our lives, we can rebuild.

Part of the overall civil defense strategy that we are proposing is the use of underground storage tanks that contain basic supplies. There would be one group of tanks for every ten human shelters. These tanks will contain such items as simple agricultural tools, dehydrated food (mainly grain and beans), water, hand tools, non-hybrid seeds, and similar basic survival equipment. (See Appendix 4)

People would have to avoid any actual bomb craters for an extended period. These craters would remain dangerously radioactive for months after the blast. Other than this, the levels of radioactivity in the environment would be safe in a short time.

Radioactivity in fallout decays rapidly. For each seven-fold increase in time, there is a ten-fold decrease in radiation. Therefore, if in a high fallout area the radiation level were 2000 R/day one hour after an attack, it would be 200 R/day after seven hours, 20 R/day after two days, and 2 R/day after two weeks. Serious human health problems begin to appear at levels of 200 R or more total short term exposure or 3 R/day or more long-term exposure. (See Appendix 5—Radiation and Fallout.)

Around the limited areas where there had been

very high fallout, some trees and plant life, and many animals would be dead. Plant life would recover from existing seeds in the ground; animals would migrate in.

Buildings would be rubble, but not vaporized. Frame houses would be piles of broken wood. Most would not be burned, except in areas of very dense frame construction. This rubble would not be useless. It would provide building materials. Crude shelter could be constructed. Furthermore, the bomb shelters themselves would still exist. They could be used for a time to house at least a portion of the population.

By the end of the first year, it is likely that survivors would be living in shelter at least as good as the shelter enjoyed by mid-19th-century Americans. Many of us would still be doing without running water and indoor plumbing. But life would go on.

Think about it. This is the sort of shelter Dolly Parton grew up in back in Tennessee, and nobody complains that she doesn't look healthy.

Public transportation would be slow to recover. Not all roads would be gone, but some bridges, overpasses, and other vulnerable structures would be missing. Public communication would take longer to recover. Again, it would be like mid-19th-century America for most of us, except that there would still be radio communications for emergencies. It might take a generation to rebuild everything.

The nation would be decentralized overnight. So would politics. This decentralization would have its advantages. You could forget about your annual struggle with the IRS 1040 forms.

If there is any significant warning (six hours for example) machine tools and other heavy equipment can be protected. Heavy equipment is ruined primarily by being thrown over or into something or being hit by falling or flying objects. By covering the equipment with bags of metal shavings or other packing material and then bulldozing dirt over it, machine tools could be saved. (The Boeing Company conducted tests years ago that proved this.) Such equipment can be used to make other equipment.[1]

There would be shortages of meat and fresh food for two years—more, if the country were invaded militarily. We would live on grains and sprouts— rather like the diet recommended by some health food proponents.

C. Medical Care

Doctors might start making house calls again. ("Fantasy!" some readers may be thinking. "Survival after a nuclear war, maybe, but not doctors who make house calls.") Hospitals would be operating.

There is no doubt that items such as aspirin would be valuable, along with many other items of medical equipment. Anesthetics would be more valuable than gold for a time. But medical care is to a great degree based on knowledge of basic sanitation. Such knowledge would not disappear overnight.

Death by disease would increase, but most peo-

---

1. J. W. Russel and E. N. York, *Expedient Industrial Protection Against Nuclear Attack* (Seattle, Washington: Boeing, 1980).

ple have received immunization shots. Immunization would not wear off just because there had been an atomic attack.

There would still be a threat of biological warfare, but that would exist with or without shelters. Our recommended "button-up" shelters provide excellent defense against biological and chemical warfare. Shelters would still provide some protection, even after an attack. The shelters markedly improve our chances of survival in an age of murderous totalitarian governments.

D. Bureaucracies

Most lawyers and bureaucrats would have to go to work at something more economically productive. This is one of the positive aspects of nuclear war: fewer paper shufflers. We would have market competition and tougher performance standards.

E. Mortality

In that first "year after," there could be an additional increase in deaths above today's peacetime normal rate, although even this may not happen. It would depend on such factors as weather, disease, people's attitudes, and so forth

Much of life and death in a crisis depends on a person's attitude toward life. Some people will not be able to face a world without today's conveniences. They may prefer to die. On the other hand, if we are correct about our perception of most Americans, we would expect a transformation of people's moral and spiritual condition. We would expect a new dedication to life, a new dedication to life that today's easier life does not encourage. We think a post-attack society would encourage courage.

Mentally tough people would survive in greater proportions. People with faith in God and the future would be more likely to survive. People who value freedom and justice and hate tyranny and evil would be more likely to survive. People who continue to define life mainly in terms of luxury and creature comforts would suffer higher death rates.

F. People

The key to rebuilding society is people. The key to people's survival after a war will be their attitudes and a minimal capital base. The major capital base is knowledge and a willingness to cooperate, not bricks and mortar.

If people are alive to rebuild, they *will* rebuild. The world a year after will be a place very different from what it is today, and so will the rebuilt world. What we take for granted today will become luxuries. What we ignore today or think we can do without— life-and-death cooperation, real neighborhood communities, faithfulness, the work ethic, laws that punish criminal behavior—will become very important.

II. Surrender

Let us assume the following scenario. The federal government builds no shelters for its citizens. It continues to spend its funds on approximately the same programs that it spends money on today. No fundamental change in defensive strategy takes place. The strategists continue to rely on "mutual assured destruction" (MAD).

The Soviet Union could demand that the U.S. surrender by simply ordering the President to do something he didn't want to do.

What if he refuses? Then they launch a first strike against our Minuteman III missiles in their silos and our airfields. Five minutes into the launch —20 minutes to impact—the Soviet Premier calls the President on the hot line and informs him that the U.S. radar and satellite information is correct, an attack has begun. He also reminds the President that the coastal areas of the U.S. are targeted by the missiles on Soviet submarines. These submarines will launch their missiles the moment a single Minuteman III missile or U.S. submarine ballistic missile is launched.

(What this means, just for the record, is that our Minuteman III missiles are just about useless except as retaliatory devices aimed at the bomb shelters of the Soviet elite. They cannot do anything offensively to reduce the number of missiles that will strike the U.S. They are simply psychological devices to instill fear in the Soviet leaders. The day the Soviets think they can survive such an attack, the Minuteman III missiles—this nation's primary weapon system—will be close to useless.)

Or the President can do nothing and allow the Minuteman III missiles to be destroyed. Perhaps ten million Americans would die, or perhaps more, depending on fallout patterns.

What will the President do? It is fairly easy to

guess. He will not call for the launching of the Minuteman III missiles. Fifteen minutes later: boom—no more land-based missiles and bombers. Then he will be told to call back all U.S. submarines to their ports. He will be instructed to disarm them.

Simple, isn't it? Risky for the Soviets—he might call for the launch—but simple. Sometime in 1987, the Soviets should have their huge phased-array radar system operational, and their anti-ballistic missile system will then be secured. Not many of our missiles will be able to strike Soviet targets. The Soviets will thereby reduce their risk of retaliation, even if the President gets half the Minuteman missiles launched. Submarine commanders may or may not launch their missiles.

In our view, this is the Soviet Union's major risk: the individual decisions of a few submarine commanders who have been widowers for an hour or so. But submarine-launched ballistic missiles are relatively small, and they are not accurate enough to strike specific buildings or Soviet leaders' shelters. Furthermore, these U.S. subs may be detected by Soviet satellites or antisubmarine ships and destroyed by a nuclear attack before they learn of the Soviet attack.

The 500 or so huge floating targets known as surface ships will no longer be in existence by this time. Surface ships don't survive nuclear wars.

In short, the President will surrender.

U.S. military troops will be disarmed. Some may make a run for the hills, but they are not trained or equipped to be guerrillas. In any case, armed protection will be removed from the cities.

Resistance

Will people in the cities resist? No one knows. Americans are heavily armed with small weapons. They may decide not to cooperate. But urban dwellers are unlikely to become guerrillas if their homes are still standing. They will probably hope for the best. They will hope to make a deal with the new Soviet-controlled government.

People who have seen their homes destroyed and who have experienced two weeks in a crowded shelter will have a far different mentality from newly conquered middle-class people who are terrified of losing what they have and who are only vaguely aware of what Communist governments do to newly conquered civilians. Members of the latter group will be far less ready to resist. They will assume that "it may not be that bad; we can always go along to get along."

Then the executions will begin, just as they have begun in every country that the Soviets have captured. This time, however, there will be no world opinion to consider. World opinion is no more powerful than the United States' ability to constrain the Soviets. Once the United States is eliminated, the Nice Guy image of the Soviets will disappear. They will start getting *really* mean.

There will be very few paper-shuffling, eight-hour-a-day jobs available to a typical breadwinner. If they kill as many civilians proportionally as the Communists did in Cambodia, 70 million people will be eliminated.

There are 50 million church-going Christians in the United States. These people are the primary targets of world Communism. They are Communism's greatest threat. They probably will not be tolerated. They will not be allowed to pursue their "counter-revolutionary subversive activities." They will not be allowed "to corrupt the minds of the youth," meaning their own children. They will not be allowed to do these things—Christians will be *exterminated*.

We estimate that as many people will be executed as would have perished in a medium-level atomic attack if we do not build shelters. But you and I will never know for sure. They won't be taking a census soon, and we wouldn't be around to read it anyway.

Perhaps the one-by-one executions will never begin. The Soviets may decide to nuke us anyway, once we call back the subs. Or they may use some of the 300,000 tons of chemical and biological weapons that they have in storage in Cuba and elsewhere.

The U.S. border will be opened to every terrorist group under Communist control. The "Red Dawn" scenario could easily become a reality. But teenage kids with stolen machine guns will not defeat well-trained Cuban or Soviet troops that know all about guerrilla operations. It looks good in the movies; it won't be as easy to defeat them as it looked on screen.

Conclusion
The year after a full-scale first strike, if we have no shelters, most of the occupants of North America will be Spanish-speaking. They will operate under

Russian military and political leaders. Surviving English-speaking Americans will be slaves.

The year after a surrender by the President, this may also be the case. Or we could see a diminishing population of Americans living in fear and waiting for a knock at the door. We will be slaves to the most ferocious, murderous tyrants in history.

The year after a full-scale strike against Americans with shelters, most Americans will still be alive. Perhaps they will be fighting an invading army. Perhaps not. But any invader will face far greater resistance than if the attack had come against people with no shelters.

Finally, *the year after the installation of shelters, there may be no visible changes at all.* The very existence of the shelters will make a blackmail strategy much more risky to the Soviets. The backbone of Americans will be stronger, and this will help any President to resist. The will to resist will be greatly strengthened. The Soviets will have more and more to fear from the resistance of surviving Americans. The shelters will change the Soviet strategy. There will be no more free rides for Soviet strategists.

The shelters will give us the position of strength that the Chinese possess today. The very fact that they cannot be annihilated makes the Soviets' missile-rattling less effective. The Soviets don't rattle their missiles more loudly today, because they fear that Americans will begin taking effective defensive action before they are ready for the final countdown.

If we fail to defend ourselves while the Soviets act like pussycats, we will soon be attacked by the ultimate tiger. Only a miracle will prevent this if we refuse to defend ourselves.

Part III
FOOT DRAGGING

8

"IT'S NOT WASHINGTON'S RESPONSIBILITY!"

Washington's latest political line on civil defense is that each individual needs to look out for himself. It's the responsibility of every family to design and then build a bomb shelter if a family really wants one.

The politicians, of course, expect us to protect *them*. In May 1986 the Federal Emergency Management Agency, FEMA, proposed a $1.5 billion program to build shelters for the "essential" national, state, and local *politicians and bureaucrats*. For the taxpayers, however, FEMA proposed a do-it yourself approach without public shelters or expenditures. They want us to pay for shelters only for some adults — the same adults who have decided not to protect our kids, our soldiers, and ourselves!

Let's look at this Party Line in greater detail. Consider the following analogies:

1. People want street lights. Let them install

them themselves, house by house. The government has no responsibility here.

2. People want roads. Let families pour the concrete themselves, house by house. The government has no responsibility here.

3. People want police protection. Let them hire private policemen, block by block. The government has no responsibility here.

4. People want an army and a navy to defend the nation. Let each family rent and train a soldier or a sailor. The government has no responsibility here.

5. People want a strategic defense system. Let them set up a non-profit foundation and donate money to build the system, or, perhaps each neighborhood should install its own phased-array radar and ABM launcher. The government has no responsibility here.

Crazy, aren't they? Absolutely ridiculous. Then comes the new Party Line in Washington:

People want protection from a Soviet attack with 10,000 or more nuclear warheads. Let each concerned family design and build its own bomb shelter. The government has no responsibility here.

This is just as crazy. Do you know anyone who knows how to design a bomb shelter? Do you know of a single U.S. firm that produces a commercially available blast door? (We said U.S. firm, not Swiss.)

Do you know anyone who will accept the ridicule that will be heaped on him if he builds a shelter all by himself? Do you know any city where the planning commission won't fine someone who starts building a shelter that hasn't been approved by a team of bureaucrats and zoned properly? Of course you don't. But the bureaucrats in Washington say that it is now your responsibility to build a home-brew blast shelter for your family.

This, believe it or not, is the official line. Civil defense officials are required to operate in terms of it. They don't come before the public (meaning Congress) and argue in favor of immediate deployment of a full-scale, Washington-financed civil defense blast shelter system. We are unaware of any hearings before Congress in the last twenty years in which any full-time, government-employed civil defense official testified that the government should build a comprehensive blast shelter system for the American people. Yet in private, they say it needs to be done. They are too fearful or too demoralized after 30 years of failure to say it in public. The public is kept in the dark.

During World War II, the German government built bunkers for public air raids. The bunkers prevented casualties to their occupants, except in very rare instances. However, construction of these shelters was started too late, so part of the German population was sheltered in civilian-made, home-brew shelters in their basements and elsewhere. The people in these amateur shelters suffered horrible mass casualties, especially during the mass bombings, which had effects similar to modern nuclear weapons. Home-brew shelters turned out to be do-it-yourself death traps.

Hermits and Survival

The genius of modern economics is that we all buy services and goods from each other. We use the *division of labor* to increase our wealth as individuals. Each person contributes something to the system.

Anyone knows that if he alone survives, he won't survive long. *We need each other to maintain our lives.* If we can help each other, we can rebuild. The Amish cooperate with each other, and the Mennonites cooperate with each other. The zero-debt farms of both groups are very productive. The Amish may use horses and buggies, but they are buying up bankrupt mechanized farms all over Pennsylvania, cash on the line. They have real communities. They have community spirit.

What about the rest of us? Is anyone so stupid that he would imagine that he could survive in a post-attack world all by himself? Does he think that his own personal productivity could sustain his family if all his neighbors were dead? Such thinking is so ridiculous that only a bureaucrat in Washington could operate in terms of it. Few people are going to build shelters for their families if they know that their neighbors won't do it, too. Why bother? Without our neighbors, we can't hope to do much more than barely survive for a few months or years. We need each other.

So we ask Congress to protect us — all of us. And

what do they tell us? Something that is implicitly little different from the following.

Dear Sir:

Recently you wrote to me about funding a national system of bomb shelters. My recommendation to you is that if you really are so foolish as to believe that the peace-loving Soviet Union would do anything so rash as to launch an atomic attack against the United States, thereby wiping out our missiles and our people, and opening up the whole country to invasion, well, you can continue to live in a dream world. I know better. Build your own shelter. You're on your own. Tax money is needed for important things, not national survival. We need the money to guarantee more low-interest loans to Poland.

Very sincerely,
Martin J. Dealer
U.S. Senate

If we try to survive alone, the handful of survivors will not survive long. Do-it-yourself protection from a nuclear war is the most ridiculous idea to come out of Washington in thirty years.

Invasion

Can you imagine how you would defend the nation against a hundred thousand or more Cuban soldiers, plus ten or twenty divisions of Soviet soldiers? If this nation were hit by 5,000 to 10,000 or more atomic warheads (depending on how many they have and how many they hold in reserve), and 90 percent of the population perished (including our ground-based armed forces) because the federal government was too cheap to buy us protection, do you think your family could hold off a trained army?

If we can keep most of our people alive, and if our armed forces have shelters, too, then we have a fighting chance. The people who climb out of those shelters will be fighting mad. Any invader will have a problem subduing us. If they use chemical or biological warfare, we'll go back into the shelters and button up again until the weapons are impotent. If they try to subdue us, they will meet resistance.

But if 90 percent of us are dead, the land will fill up with invaders, and then other Spanish-speaking people will simply walk 30 days north and inherit our land. These people will then come under communist domination. They will probably serve as agrarian and mine labor for the Soviets.

We have nothing against Spanish-speaking citizens. We are simply looking at a map. Highly productive open land won't remain open forever. If the Soviets soften us up with a first strike that kills most of our people, we can't protect ourselves. We desperately need something to offset this threat. We need a wild card that will upset their plans. That wild card is a workable civil defense shelter system.

The scientists know the system will work, technically speaking. If people respond to occasional drills, and if they take the threat seriously, the system could save almost 200 million lives. It could give us a backbone again. The President wouldn't have to knuckle under in the face of Soviet nuclear blackmail. (He might knuckle under anyway, but he wouldn't have to. These days, he hasn't much choice. We have no protection.)

So why won't Congress give us the shelters we need that will give them the political backbone they need?

Conclusion

We're not facing an unsolvable technical problem. We're facing a "leadership backbone" problem.

Most Americans simply don't know what the threat really is. They think the technological threat is so big— "everyone on earth will be killed"—that no one will ever start a nuclear war. They have overestimated the technological threat and underestimated the strategic threat. If they had not been misled by their leaders and the media, they would stand and fight. Or better put, they would demand protection from bombs, so that they could offer effective resistance to invaders. They would make invaders pay a high price for every inch of ground. They would end the free ride that our government has given our mortal enemies.

It's tough to show much backbone after it has been vaporized by a nuclear explosion. If we have no shelters, any talk about showing backbone is not going to be taken seriously.

The idea that the protection of American civilians from an atomic attack is the personal, individual responsibility of adult family members, house by house, block by block, is an idea dreamed up by time-serving bureaucrats who have nothing to offer in return for their $60,000 a year salaries.

It is simple: the civil defense bureaucrats must fight for the implementation of an effective program, or they ought to be put behind desks in Guam until they retire. Thirty years of not protecting the public is an act of irresponsibility exceeded only by generals who will not put their careers on the line for the sake of getting shelters for their troops. They should be retired early if they cannot legally be fired. Thirty years of lies, particularly lies of omission, about the threat we have faced is inexcusable. At least they could have warned us clearly; at least they could have sounded a trumpet:

> For if the trumpet give an uncertain sound, who shall prepare himself for the battle? (I Corinthians 14:8).

9

SLOGANS AGAINST
CIVIL DEFENSE

We need to consider the kinds of arguments that opponents of civil defense might offer. It seems incredible that people would have objections to a system of protective shelters that could give us a way to reduce the threat against us. The Red Chinese understand that a nation cannot keep its national independence free of charge. So do the Swiss. So do the Soviets. But opponents of civil defense have successfully foiled any attempt to use tax money to protect Americans from nuclear attack.

Some of the following arguments are never really stated openly. Nobody really wants to admit that he believes them. They are just too ridiculous. But in the back of the minds of our elected representatives, something like these arguments must be hidden. If they weren't, why wouldn't they have built our shelters back in 1964 or 1965? For that matter, why not in the 1950s?

If a proposal to build a civil defense system

should begin to be actively discussed by television commentators and newspaper editorial writers, we can expect to hear versions of the following arguments. Be prepared for arguments that "We don't need to be prepared for the Soviets."

The Soviets Don't Want War, So We Don't Need Shelters

Why have they built more than 10,000 nuclear warheads and a first-strike delivery system? Why do they have an army of 195 divisions, plus an additional 20 KGB and MVD secret police divisions, for a total of 215, when the United States has only 16? Why do they teach the first-strike nuclear strategy in their military manuals? Why do they repeat in their published strategic planning that a nuclear war can be won? Why are they deploying a new generation of mobile-launched missiles that cannot be attacked by the West's missiles?

Of course, they don't want war *if* they can get us to surrender without a war. Whatever follows a U.S. surrender to the Soviet Union isn't war. It's called genocide. It's also called slaughter. At the very least, it's called slavery. It's called the victory of proletariat forces over the capitalist imperialists.

In Afghanistan, the Soviets place what appear to be toys close to villages. When small children pick them up, the toys explode. These toys are sometimes called butterfly bombs, because they resemble toy butterflies. The explosions are designed to blow off the children's hands, not kill them. The children become permanent visible testimonies to Soviet ruthlessness. In short, the Soviets believe in terror.

The threat of nuclear war is pure, unadulterated terror. They can threaten us with terror any time they please. We can't threaten them with anything, least of all the survival of our people.

Technically, we don't have a fighting chance.

If We Build Shelters, They Will Attack Us

See the preceding assurance: "The Soviets Don't Want War." Then read Chapter 12.

Building Shelters Will De-Stabilize International Relations

Imagine that a bully is about to knock your teeth out. He has said for years that he intends to do it. He bought some brass knuckles. He is wearing them. He is standing in front of you. He pulls back his fist. You put your hands in front of your face.

"Stop!" a policeman shouts. "Put your hands at your sides!" You think the policeman is shouting at the bully. No, he's shouting at you. "You're just making him angry. You're going to upset him. Do the smart thing. Give him a taxpayer-subsidized loan."

But you have a sneaking suspicion that if you put your hands down and keep them at your sides, he's going to knock your teeth out. And you also have a sneaking suspicion that the policeman is scared to death of the bully.

This is a silly analogy. It's ridiculous. We admit it. It isn't nearly threatening enough. The bully is actually carrying a shotgun. It's aimed at you, and twenty people are lying dead in the street. The policeman is carrying a night stick. And you're not putting your hands in front of your face; you're trying to hide behind a wall.

Silly you. Don't you know that the wall will upset him? Don't you know that if he even thinks you plan to build a wall, he will shoot? So stand still. Smile. Tell him you'll loan him some more money. Tell him you'll make a deal, just like the policeman recommends.

Is it comforting to know that once the bully pulls the trigger and blows your head off, the next victim will be that gutless policeman? It really isn't comforting, but at least it offers a little satisfaction.

The authors of this book are tired of being protected by policemen who are afraid of the bully. It's one thing to be scared, even if you're a policeman. It's another thing for the policemen to tell us that they are fully armed, fully prepared to defend us, and a match for any bully on the block.

And every time the bully appears, our policemen take the bully out to dinner, pick up the tab, and charge it to our national credit card. This doesn't build confidence in policemen.

Building Shelters Is Almost an Act of War

Switzerland has built shelters for its people. Would you say that Switzerland plans to go to war with the Soviet Union? In Switzerland, shelters are an act of survival leading to peace and safety.

Red China has built shelters for its people. Would you say that Red China plans to go to war with the Soviet Union? The Soviets think so. In Red

China, shelters are an act of survival.

The United States has built no shelters for its people. This is an act of illusion leading to eventual annihilation or slavery.

The mere presence of shelters tells us nothing about intentions of those who built them. The absence of shelters tells a great deal about those who refuse to build them.

Maybe the Soviets Will Just Leave Us Alone

Tell it to Afghanistan. Tell it to Poland. Tell it to Eastern Europe. Tell it to someone who is totally ignorant of the history of the Soviet Union. Don't tell it to us. Tyrant states don't build over 10,000 nuclear warheads and overwhelming military superiority in order to leave their potential victims alone.

The Civil Defense Shelter System Might Not Work

Pretend that you hear the sirens. *Now* what precisely is your recommended system? You can:

1. Get on the floor of your house and await an explosion which will put up to 50 to 200 pounds or more of pressure on every square inch of its walls. Don't get in front of any windows. Stay away from flying doors, too. Sit tight. (Some system!)
2. Hide in the basement, if you have one. The initial nuclear radiation will kill every unshielded person within three miles, but you hope for the best. Then comes fallout. (Some system!)

3. Write your Congressman. Ask him to vote for a shelter program. Then again, maybe you'd better phone. He may not be there, either. He may be in the basement under Capitol Hill, wishing it had blast doors.

From a strictly technical viewpoint, a shelter system could easily save the lives of 80 percent of all Americans, if we had as little as a 15-minute warning. If we had a 25-minute warning, shelters could save over 90 percent.

Even if we had no warning, it still would be a better system than what we have now.

Remember, in the worst possible surprise attack, the Soviets will launch all missiles simultaneously. The submarine-launched missiles will hit first within ten or fifteen minutes. They will almost certainly be aimed at military targets and Washington, D.C. These explosions will alert surviving Americans to the war, even if the sirens are silent.

We don't have anything now. A three-hour warning would do no good for anyone if the Soviets launch a full-scale attack on the whole country. The fallout will kill us if the explosions don't. And the highways will look just like they do in those nuclear war movies: bumper to bumper.

No civil defense system can guarantee the survival of people who refuse to head for a shelter when they are alerted by sirens that an attack is imminent. It can't guarantee the survival of everyone in the downtown district of New York City and Chicago on a weekday, but it can save most of them. It would save most of our children. Even in the worst case, it would save more people than will be saved if there are no shelters at all.

Today, there are no shelters at all, except for some of the highest federal government officials, and even these may not do them any good.

Shelters *will* work, but only if people are inside them when the bombs explode. Any overall system of civil defense will have failings, just as every human plan has failings. This is hardly an argument for having no plan at all.

The air raid sirens surely won't save anyone.

The System Is Too Expensive

Right. We just can't afford $300 per person: $200 for the shelter and $100 for food, tools, and seeds for rebuilding. It would break the American economy.

The Red Chinese, some of the poorest people on earth, have built a tunnel system far better and more expensive (because of labor costs) than our recommended minimal shelter program. The Swiss have also built a truly first-class shelter system. The Soviets have protected their people. But it's just too expensive for Americans. We're just too poor.

In the meantime, the government spends a trillion dollars a year on "really important things."

The hour you hear the sirens, and the newscasters tell you to take cover, think about how much money you saved. Tell your kids how thrifty you've been. "Daddy, what are we going to do?" And you can answer: "We're going to die, kids (probably a death of prolonged terrible suffering), but at least I saved 300 bucks apiece. That paid for last summer's vacation to Florida. Think of all the fun we had. Think of Disney World. Think of Fantasyland. That was our favorite place: Fantasyland. But don't bother to think about Tomorrowland."

There are people who worry because the year after a nuclear attack might look like Frontierland. They think they would prefer to give up Tomorrowland in order to avoid Frontierland. They praise the frontier optimism and hard work of the people who built this nation, yet they are literally scared to death —a no-shelters death—of the possibility of rebuilding the country after an attack. They watch with great idealism television programs like "Little House on the Prairie," and yet they are fearful of a few months of life in such a setting. This is the death-rattle of paper-shufflers. If they continue to get their way, we may all die with them.

Our problem isn't technical. Our problem isn't even financial. *Our problem is spiritual.* Some of us have lost our vision and our backbones. Some of us think life isn't worth living if, during and for a while after an attack, it isn't lived in an air conditioned three-bedroom home.

If we don't stop thinking this way soon, we may not survive. The Hebrew slaves of Moses' generation were scared to death of dying in the wilderness, so God let all of them except Caleb and Joshua die in the wilderness. God gave the slaves what they feared most. Slaves live in fear. They die that way, too.

Are we afraid of nuclear war and the difficulties of rebuilding after a nuclear war? Then we had better learn the lesson of the Exodus generation. If you deliberately, self-consciously refuse to do what is morally required, God turns you over to your greatest fear in life.

It Will Take Years to Set Up the System

Yes, it will: about two years. *If* we poke along. Or more to the point, if Congress stalls the program. It will take forever if Congress votes the way Congress has voted over the last thirty years.

What's the problem? The shelters will be identical. Every American gets access to the same kind of protection. The shelters can be mass produced on American assembly lines and in local steel fabrication shops. The steel will be easily available: our steel factories are lying idle all over the Northeast.

Farmers are going broke with low grain prices; they have at least a year's supply on hand. We can stockpile the wheat in storage tanks under the ground instead of stockpiling it in grain bins above ground. We need a year's supply of wheat, but not above ground on the farms. We need it buried in steel containers ten feet under, near our homes.

What's the problem? The shelter sites are fairly easy to pick: school playgrounds and fields; city parks; public parking lots; parking lots in shopping malls. The various governments already own most of the necessary land. If we offer a bonus system, the counties will race ahead.

Red China in less than a decade did much more than this with nothing but picks and shovels, digging tunnels 30 feet below the ground and over 20 miles long. Yet the U.S. supposedly can't dig holes in the ground for underground shelters in a couple of years? Local steel fabricating plants don't need business?

If there were a war going on, would we try our best to build the shelters? Of course. Well, there *is* a war on. The trouble is, nobody in the U.S. wants to admit it. The Communists have admitted it boldly since 1917, but we don't believe them. Neither did the leaders of Poland, Lithuania, Latvia, Czechoslovakia, Cambodia, Afghanistan, Cuba, and other assorted victims. The leaders always know better. They always think that they can work out a deal with the Soviets.

The only deal you get from the Communists is dealt from the bottom of the deck.

No more deals. Deals have bought the Soviets the time that they needed. Deals gave them the missile technology which they needed to attack us. Deals have made a handful of American deal-doers rich, but they have put our necks on the chopping block. We don't have much more time. *No more deals!*

Deals indicate that we've already surrendered in principle. This is a bad message to send to a bully.

You're Trying to Build "Fortress America"
Tell it to General Custer, buddy.

There comes a time when it's nice to have something solid between you and the Indians. Those arrows can hurt. The same is true about one-megaton bombs. Ten feet of dirt and a steel tank between you and the bomb is comforting.

Illusions are also comforting, until the day the

sirens sound. Then illusions prove deadly. Americans have lived with illusions for too long. They have lived without shelters for too long. Let's trade in some illusions and buy ourselves some shelters.

You Would Stack People Up Like Cordwood

There are only two kinds of cordwood after an atomic attack: stacked-up cordwood (living) or blasted and irradiated cordwood (dead).

This is a variation of "People will be jammed together like sardines." You can figure out your own response.

We have leaders who think you wouldn't be willing to spend two weeks in a "subway car" in order to save your life. They think it would be too frightening for your children to go through this experience; they think it is better to allow Soviet generals to hold your children as hostages to nuclear terror. They think building "subway cars" for us is too expensive.

These elected representatives used your tax money to build themselves the most expensive subway in U.S. history — the ten-billion-dollar Washington, D.C. subway system (ten billion 1977 purchasing-power dollars!) — but they didn't bother to put blast doors on it and install a filtered ventilation system. An extra few million dollars spent then, when the city was dug up anyway, could save the lives today of almost everyone in the city. (In fact, that $10 billion would have bought blast shelters and post-attack supplies for over 30 million Americans.)

They could install blast protection now, but it would cost a lot more than it would have cost originally. But they refuse to spend this extra money even to save their own skins and the skins of their staff members, the bureaucrats, and city residents. Why? Because they would have to admit to the rest of the country that people need protection from the Soviet Union.

These elected officials brought their families to a prime nuclear target, and they have left their own families undefended. The few shelters that they have built for themselves require evacuation time that will probably not be available.

How enthusiastic do you think they'll be when you ask them to spend some money this year to save *your* skin? Be ready for a lot of mumbling and delays. Be ready for a lot of computerized form letters. Be ready for a lot of excuses.

Political excuses are not very useful during an atomic attack.

We Need More Time to Study the Problem

This is the last-ditch effort to stall any program that politicians don't like.

The fact is, everything we need to know was already known by the civil defense professionals when President Kennedy was in office. That's why he wanted to go ahead with the civil defense program. Unfortunately, he was killed before he could get the idea translated into action.

In the library of the Oak Ridge National Laboratory, there are 3,000 scientific and engineering articles on the subject of civil defense. The staff members at Oak Ridge have set aside 1,000 of these articles as the most significant. The basic information has been sorted out for three decades. The story is old: *Americans can be defended effectively by simple, inexpensive shelters.*

Look, a hole in the ground isn't some high-technology miracle. A steel tank inside the hole and covered with ten feet of dirt isn't anything spectacular. The scientists know exactly how powerful a nuclear weapon is when exploded above ground for maximum devastation. These shelters will keep everyone inside alive. There isn't any scientific debate about this.

So why debate about it forever? Let's settle it this year. Ask your Congressman if he thinks you're worth defending. If he doesn't, let him start worrying about how he's going to defend himself at the next election.

Conclusion

The problem facing Congress isn't a lack of knowledge. It's *a failure of nerve.* Before God, we need to change. It's time for us to say that Americans deserve a fighting chance.

"Us" means *you.* If you sit there silently, you have implicitly accepted one or more of these false slogans as the truth. You have "bought the no-protection package," hook, line, and sinker. You have tied your future and your children's future to an illusion. You have closed your eyes to what the Soviets say they can do and say they will do: *win.*

When the air raid sirens go off, you had better have steel tanks in a ten-foot hole to jump into. If you don't, your silence today will become permanent silence. Dead people can't write their Congressmen. Dead Congressmen can't send back computerized form letters, either.

Even Congressmen deserve a fighting chance.

Send him a letter or a telegram. Send one to each of your U.S. Senators, too.

And if even this is too much to ask, then tear out the "Dear Congressman" form letter at the back of this book, sign your name, put it in an envelope, and send it to him. Remember, if you don't remember his name, you can get it from the research department of your local public library. Just call them.

Part IV
THE MORAL RESPONSE

10

THE WILL TO RESIST

Let's get one fact straight from the beginning: the best way to avoid a nuclear war is to convince the Soviet Union that we will survive it. The best way to assure a surrender or a war (or even both) is to let them believe we won't survive an atomic attack.

Let's get something else clear: *a nation without shelters will not survive an atomic war.* That is to say, its people and its buildings will not survive. Its farm areas, forests, and minerals will survive quite well. In a full-scale Soviet attack, a large percentage of the U.S. population would be dead within a month. Those whom the initial blasts didn't kill, the radiation from fallout would. The country will collapse and surrender—if there is any government official still alive to surrender.

The land would survive. The invaders would easily walk into the largest piece of valuable, developed rural real estate in the history of man. And the terror of what happened to us would give them Western civilization on a silver platter.

With a little risk to the initiators—a declining amount of risk—it can be done in less than 30 minutes.

One can argue that the Soviets would only attack our military installations. If they did, we might only lose a few hundred thousand people or we might lose over 50 million people. Nobody knows for sure. The rest would surrender.

But of course, this is a questionable scenario. The President might surrender in the name of the people. The leaders might surrender in order to avoid a full strike against the cities, but the Soviets might have a real problem in subduing an outraged, armed population. Americans are the most heavily armed people in the world, except for the Swiss.

To make certain that the occupying forces did not encounter such resistance, the Soviets might well decide to launch a full-scale attack. They may regard the raw real estate as far more valuable than buildings plus armed, outraged Americans. They may not believe that certain groups speak for the rest of us with the slogan "better Red than dead." They may realize that for their long-term plans, "better dead than Red" is safer for them in their dealings with Americans, especially those Americans who are deeply religious and who see themselves as responsible before God for defending a civilization built originally on God's law.

It is undoubtedly true that they don't target civilians with all of their missiles. They no doubt do have one strategy to blow up our Minuteman III missiles in their silos in a first strike, leaving civilian populations alone, but it is unlikely that this is their only strategy. They are careful strategists. They have devised many ways to subdue their enemies militarily. They are masters of such techniques.

A good way to reduce future guerrilla resistance is to annihilate in advance most of the people who might otherwise become guerrillas.

Blackmail

Without shelters for the U.S. population, the Soviets might be able to blackmail our leaders into surrendering without ever launching an attack. We might not even know about the surrender until it is irreversible. Selling out our allies in South Africa, Europe, Asia, and Central America might be carried out under Soviet orders to our leaders — and made to appear as reasonable, independent actions in our press.

In a substantial sense, our government's present fear that *deployment* of civil defense and *deployment* of strategic defense must be delayed, so that we will not anger or worry the Soviets, is itself a kind of implicit surrender. This policy, if continued, could easily lead eventually to actual surrender. We think it *will* lead to surrender, or nuclear annihilation.

That's why this policy must be reversed. Soon.

Also, the money and technology that are provided to the Soviets are a kind of "surrender" (although "treason" might be a more accurate word). The U.S. government encourages U.S. banks to give the Soviets and their satellites long-term loans at interest rates far below those at which they loan money to

Americans. About $80 billion was loaned to them in the 1970s at interest rates more favorable than American businesses could receive,[1] with over $20 billion of this money going to economically hopeless Poland. A branch of government, the Export-Import Bank, was established to use taxpayers' money to guarantee the repayment of such cheap loans, just in case the Soviets default. Your money would be used to pay off the lending banks. Harvard scholar Richard Pipes explains:

> The debt of the Soviet Union to Western assistance is not widely known, because neither of the parties involved wishes to advertise it — the Soviet Union wants to avoid the embarrassment of conceding that it is more or less permanently dependent on the "capitalist camp," while Western firms are coy about doing business with a power that most Westerners view as hostile and spend great sums to arm themselves against. (To this day, the U.S. Department of Commerce will not release lists of industrial corporations granted export licenses to the Soviet Union, although such business is perfectly legitimate.)[2]

Perfectly legal, yes. Perfectly legitimate? Not in our view!

---

1. Richard Pipes, *Survival Is Not Enough: Soviet Realities and America's Future* (New York: Simon & Schuster, 1984), p. 261.
2. *Ibid.*, p. 260.

There is even a nearly secret, not-for-profit corporation that makes it easier for big, big U.S. firms to do business in the Soviet Union. Its membership list is secret. The government won't release the names, and the organization certainly won't. Their hundreds of corporate members insist on secrecy. It's called the US-USSR Trade and Economic Council. They even publish a small-circulation magazine, *The Journal of the US-USSR Trade and Economic Council.* You can't subscribe to it, but members of the Council can. Its address is 805 Third Avenue, New York, New York, 10022. The Soviets write most of the articles, and the Americans run most of the ads. And it's our guess that the participating American corporations deduct the cost of running these ads from their taxable income at the end of the year. If they do, then you get to make up this shortfall in tax revenues.

The Soviets are our mortal enemies. We have a $300 billion annual defense budget which supposedly is spent to protect us from these mortal enemies. Then we turn around and feed them, and we sell them the technology that makes possible their future victory.

Most Americans have never been told that U.S. tax money in 1966 paid for the construction of the roads that led from the Soviet Union into Afghanistan, right into the capital of Kabul. The Soviets even helped build them.[3] Do you wonder why? When

---

3. "Rugged Afghan Road Jobs Fill Gap in Trans-Asian Network," *Engineering News Record* (Nov. 3, 1966).

those Soviet tanks roll across Afghanistan, there ought to be signs in Russian along the highways: "U.S. Highway Tax Dollars at Work." The Soviet tanks and trucks themselves were made, in part, with facilities that were built by American corporations and financed by American banks.

Most Americans have never been told that a U.S. company, the Bryant Chucking Grinder Company of Springfield, Vermont, in 1972 sold the Soviet Union the ball bearing machines that made possible the guidance system of MIRV'ed warhead missiles. (MIRV stands for "multiple independently targeted re-entry vehicle": many warheads per missile, each precisely accurate.) The Soviets had tried from 1961 to 1972 to buy these machines (Centalign-B grinders), but they were prohibited from buying them by the U.S. government. The Soviets therefore couldn't make any MIRV'ed missiles. Then, in 1972, the Nixon administration suddenly authorized the sale.[4] The Bryant Company presumably made millions. It has cost us taxpayers hundreds of billions. It will cost us everything if they use those MIRV'ed missiles before we get our shelters built.

Why don't we have shelters? Keep asking yourself this important question. One answer is ridiculous: "We don't need them." Find another answer.

Psychological Prisoners

Without shelters, our leaders are psychological prisoners. They know that the Soviets can kill almost all of us. To resist any evil, you have to be alive. It is very difficult to imagine how a successful resistance

---

4. Pipes, *Survival Is Not Enough*, p. 264.

effort could be sustained if your enemy has the technical power to kill you at any time. How does one resist totalitarian evil in such a world?

Provide bomb shelters for all 235 million Americans, and then we can begin to discuss our survival. But the government refuses to provide the shelters. So we don't resist. Neither do our leaders. We have become prisoners of power because we first became *prisoners of mental defeat*.

The absence of shelters makes the will to resist appear to be an exercise in futility, *if you don't believe in God*. A lot of our nation's senior advisors operate as though they don't believe in God. Furthermore, a lot of Christians act as though they don't believe that God offers us earthly means to achieve His will, and we mean *earthly* means: ten feet under the earth.

Atheists who are ready to surrender (or make more deals) think that God can't protect us, and that it's too late for building shelters. A lot of Christians think that God will automatically protect us, so it's unnecessary to build shelters. The authors of this book think that God can and will protect us, but in order for Him to take us seriously, we had better do what is in our power to do: build shelters. "The Lord helps those who help themselves." Benjamin Franklin said that, and he was on sound theological ground. If we don't care enough to do whatever we can to build the will to resist evil, then why should God intervene? Our problem isn't technical ignorance. Our problem isn't that we have no money to build shelters.

What is our problem? *Our problem is that our politicians have lost the will to resist*. Maybe the voters have lost it, too. If we haven't, then we must pressure our political representatives to build shelters that will help protect us.

Anyone who has the will to resist will seek to protect his life and his family's lives. He will also try to protect his neighbor's life. We cannot hope to survive as isolated individuals. We will either "hang together or hang separately."

Some people look at semi-independent and tiny Finland, which borders the U.S.S.R., and hope that we too could get along with the Soviet Union if we are willing to give in to them from time to time. These people forget that Finland had to beat the Soviets to a military draw in 1940, against overwhelming odds. They raised the price of Soviet victory too high. *But the Finns initially sought victory, not a draw.* We must not suffer from delusions. The Soviets respect power. The French commentator Revel has stated it well: "The Finns were 'Finlandized' because they resisted Sovietization with no thought of compromise. Had they said, 'Let us accept Finlandization,' they would have been Sovietized, not Finlandized."[5]

Is resistance morally justified? Of course. We find many cases of resistance throughout history that led directly to today's liberties. The revolt of the English barons against King John in 1215 led to the Magna Carta and trial by a jury of one's peers. The American Revolution is another example. The Bible provides a theology of resistance.[6]

---

5. Jean-François Revel, *How Democracies Perish* (Garden City, New York: Doubleday, 1984), p. 118.

6. Gary North (ed.), *The Theology of Christian Resistance* (Tyler, Texas: Geneva Divinity School, 1983).

Conclusion

The first political step in a program of resistance to the Soviet Union is to demand that the U.S. government provide us with *defense*. We don't have it today.

The second step is to pressure Congress to build shelters, the first stage of any military defense program. The Soviets will then have to reconsider the ease with which they can conquer us today.

If they blast us after the shelters are built, they will have to face a new kind of American. Those who survive will never forget the experience. But to survive, we need the shelters.

A completely different population would emerge from the shelters. In fact, *the very existence of the shelters would testify to an earlier transformation of the American people*. The present political leadership on both sides of the Iron Curtain, being fundamentally opposed to major changes, worries about such a transformation.

This is why a shelter system must be forced on our elected representatives by the voters. It will not come from the political leaders. This is why you must not wait for our political leaders to build a shelter system on their own initiative. They will build it only when voters make them fear the political consequences of not building it more than they fear either the budget fight or the Soviet Union. Our elected representatives have the will to resist . . . to resist the voters. We voters must break down their will to resist us. To do this, we must increase our own will to resist procrastination, political dancing, vague form letters, delays, excuses, and *other defenses of cowardice in the face of nuclear danger.*

We have to be more determined than either our elected representatives or the Soviet General Staff. To do this, we must first exercise faith in something beyond bombs, missiles, and armies.

11

THE SUICIDE SYNDROME

If your house were to catch on fire tonight, would you grab your children and run outside? Or would you sit on the floor of your bedroom and bewail the injustice of being inside a burning house?

Would you grab the kids and run even if the house weren't insured?

Would you grab the kids and run even if you could never afford to buy another house?

Would you grab your kids and run even if you had to spend the next five years in a tent?

The answer in every case is "yes," right?

Then why won't you write to your Congressman and tell him to vote to get a shelter system built for your kids immediately?

There are two main arguments that are used to oppose having the government build shelters for its people. All the other arguments are smoke screens. These two arguments are:

"I'd rather die than face a post-nuclear-war world!"

"If we start building shelters, the Soviets will attack us."

We cover the second objection in the next chapter. In this chapter, we deal with the more fundamental problem: *psychological paralysis* that is based on the suicide impulse.

Consider the Alternative

Anyone who says to himself or to anyone else, "I'd rather die than face a post-nuclear-war world!" has given up hope in this world. This world is a world in which nuclear war is a Soviet strategic reality, written into Soviet strategic planning. Nuclear war is as much a possibility as surrender to the Soviet Union. Yet we seldom hear anyone say, "I'd rather die than see the United States surrender to the Soviet Union."

The fact is, most people would be far better off to walk out of a post-attack shelter alive to face the realities of life, even including military invasion, than to live in a world in which the United States has surrendered to the Soviet Union.

Anyone who takes lightly the thought of surrendering to the Soviet Union needs to read the book by Robert Conquest and John M. White, *What to Do When the Russians Come: A Survivor's Guide*. Order a copy from your local bookstore. It was published by Stein and Day in 1984. In no-nonsense terms, they describe exactly what kind of horrors await us if this ever happens. Conquest wrote the major book on Stalin's murder of 20 million to 30 million Russians, including a million Communist Party members, in his 1968 book, *The Great Terror*. He knows what our enemies are: ruthless beyond anything in man's recorded history.

But people don't think of the very real possibility that soon the President of the United States will face a choice: surrender or be annihilated. People do occasionally think about nuclear war, and they express their total fear of this possibility. That's why, when the showdown comes, the President may surrender. He knows the hearts of the people who elected him.

Unless the people have a change of heart.

Something to Live For

The Book of Proverbs says this of those who hate God: ". . . all they that hate me love death" (Proverbs 8:36).

The Book of Psalms says this:

The right hand of the Lord is exalted: the right hand of the Lord doeth valiantly. I shall not die, but live, and declare the works of the Lord. The Lord hath chastened [punished] me sore: but he hath not given me over unto death (Psalm 118:16-18).

Right now — we mean this literally — you need to think about which verses best describe your present mental attitude. Do you love death more than a hard fight? Do you think that death is preferable to a hard life, but with the ability to declare the works of God?

If you answer "yes" to yourself, then you had better begin worrying about things a lot more important than nuclear war, American foreign policy, and similar peripheral issues. You had better start worrying about your moral character and your relationship with the God who judges eternally. Forget about this brief vail of tears; think about what you are and where you're headed. As Jesus warned: "Fear not them which kill the body, but are not able to kill the soul: but rather fear him which is able to destroy both soul and body in hell" (Matthew 10:28).

The Apostle Paul spent many years in Roman jails. It must have been depressing. Yet he wrote the most famous letters in the history of Western civilization while he was inside those prisons.

He preferred to die. But he didn't ask for death. Why not? Because he had his work to do. He had to complete his "tour of duty" in God's spiritual army. He was in service to God and to God's people. He wrote to the Philippian church:

> For I am in a strait [tight place] between two, having a desire to depart, and to be with Christ; which is far better: Nevertheless to abide in the flesh is more needful [necessary] for you (Philippians 1:23- 24).

Heaven was a nicer place than a Roman jail. But, then again, it's a nicer place than anywhere else on this sin-cursed earth, too. It's even nicer than a three-bedroom house with air conditioning. Yes, even if the mortgage is paid off! (Hard to believe, isn't it?) Heaven is supposed to come when your work is over.

What Kind of Crummy Army
Are We In, Anyway?

Why is surviving a nuclear war more frightening to people than going into the front lines to fight a military enemy? Americans are inspired by George C. Scott's delivery of a famous speech by General George Patton. The speech introduces the movie, "Patton." Patton really did give that speech (although it was saltier than the movie version). The speech calls for personal victory over fear in the face of death. He led men to their graves; any military leader who goes into battle has to see his own men die. That's the price of battle.

Parents have sent their sons off to fight, knowing that their sons may not return, and knowing surely that some parents' sons won't return. They wish their sons didn't have to go, but not to the extent that they tell their sons to run. They do not send them off with a reminder, "Son, if you face the enemy, do whatever you can to get out of the line of fire. Always try to get someone else's son to take the risks. If you see that you're sure to be killed, run. You may get court-martialed later, but the risk of a firing squad is lower than the risk of sure death at the hand of some nameless enemy."

They don't call on their sons to get killed. Instead, if they understand warfare, they echo Patton's thought: "You're job isn't to die for your country. Your job is to get the other poor, dumb bastard to die for *his* country." That's what he said, and everyone we've ever spoken to who saw the movie remembers it and agrees with it.

Yet some of those same people immediately respond to the idea of bomb shelters: "I'd rather die than face a post-nuclear-war world!"

All right, let's hear the *real* version:

"I'd rather have my children die with me, too, rather than face a post-nuclear world!"

That's exactly what that slogan means. You know it does. What else could it mean? "We shouldn't spend $300 per person in order to give us a fighting chance at survival. Forget about the kids. Life without luxury wouldn't be worth living." This slogan reminds one of Communist Jim Jones and his suicide cult.

Have they asked the kids what they think? Anyone who refuses to support the idea of civil defense because he doesn't want to survive a nuclear war is speaking in the name of his children and every other American's children.

That slogan means that it's better to see our children incinerated, or given into Soviet slavery, than to pay for some holes for us to jump into, if that evil day ever arrives.

Thought Control

Now that we've put it this way, you probably don't want to admit that Americans ever believed such a stupid, God-defying, child-destroying slogan. You're embarrassed about it. You want to take it back. You never believed it.

But some Americans do believe it. The question

is, why do they believe it?

They believe it because the enemies of the United States have pulled off one of the most successful psychological warfare operations in the history of man. It is seen most clearly in the statement by Soviet Premier Khrushchev: "The survivors will envy the dead."

He didn't believe that garbage for five seconds or a hundred billion rubles. He and his successors went out and built an excellent civil defense system for the Soviet people. They have spent a fortune to increase the likelihood that their people will be the survivors who "envy the dead." More to the point, they have done what is necessary to increase the likelihood that we in the United States will be the dead who will be "envied."

Americans have had their thoughts directed by people who really would rather take a chance with a surrender to the Soviets and who think that they will do better than all the other "leaders of opinion" who thought they could work out a deal with the Soviets. They died in prison camps or jails. But before they died, they delivered their nations into the hands of the enemy. They did it by paralyzing the average citizen through fear. "What if we don't cooperate? Life wouldn't be worth living without . . ." Without what? Fill in the blank. Whatever the citizens fear losing, that's what they'll be made to believe they can keep, if they just don't get the Soviet Union upset.

We have been the victims of a brilliant, devilish program of thought control. We have been exposed for forty years to a continuing theme: life isn't worth living after a nuclear war. Nonsense; *life is always worth living, unless it costs you your soul, your honor, or your first principles of life.* But people in the West who used to know better about what life is all about have allowed themselves to be emotionally seduced by a myth: that nothing will survive an atomic attack.

Think back to the Bible stories that made an impression on you in your youth, the stories every child seems to respond to positively. Think of Joseph in Pharaoh's prison, Daniel in the Lion's den, and every child's favorite, David and Goliath. Think of Paul in prison, alone, suffering ridicule. Think of the crucifixion of Christ. Where did each grim event lead? To victory. To resurrection.

Everyone remembers the names of the victims. Who remembers the names of the jailers, governors, and prominent citizens of the day? They are dust, forgotten. We remember only the prisoners. And Pontius Pilate. Who wants to be remembered as today's version of Pontius Pilate?

This nation was pioneered by Pilgrims and Puritans in New England and Englishmen in Virginia who experienced poverty, bad weather, and literal starvation in the early years of this nation. The men who fought the Revolution over a century later put their lives and property on the line. They paid a heavy price. Yet some of their heirs are afraid of facing a world without luxury.

The difference between a Promised Land and a wilderness is the faith and dedication of the people who inherit it. If men fear life beyond nuclear war more than they fear nuclear war itself, then they have in principle committed suicide already.

That's why this country has no nuclear blast shelters. Congress in its suicidal wisdom has reflected the suicidal hearts of some of the voters.

How could it have happened? The people who fought World War II on two fronts are afraid of surviving the next war. Not afraid of the next war—afraid of *surviving* it.

There are only three reasonable explanations.

1. We have lost our nerve.
2. We have been brainwashed.
3. Both of the above.

Let us hope that the second answer is the correct one. If it is really the first answer, then we will fall to the Soviets. It is the end of our world. At the tail end of any civilization, the people lose their nerve. It happened to the Greeks.[1] It happened to the Romans.[2] It will eventually happen to the Communists. The question is: When? Will this nation be annihilated first?

Firetrap

The other reason why Americans say to themselves that life wouldn't be worth living in the world

---

1. Gilbert Murray, *The Five Stages of Greek Religion* (New York: Doubleday Anchor, [1925] 1955), chapter 4: "The Failure of Nerve."

2. Charles Norris Cochrane, *Christianity and Classical Culture: A Study of Thought and Action From Augustus to Augustine* (New York: Oxford University Press [1944] 1957), chapter 4.

beyond nuclear war is that they see no hope to survive the initial holocaust. *Without shelters*, this perception is correct: they *won't* survive. So in mental self-defense, they implicitly say to themselves, "Since I can't do anything to survive, and since a nuclear war will destroy me and everything on earth that I hold dear, I might as well assume that it won't happen. Yet it may happen. So I'll escape from the mental anguish by telling myself and anyone who mentions nuclear war that I'd rather not survive."

We are living in a firetrap without a fire escape. If that nuclear fire comes, we *won't* be able to escape *unless we have taken steps beforehand*. But seeing no way to get the escape route built, we console ourselves with the thought that life just wouldn't be worth living after a nuclear attack. This becomes a source of the very paralysis that prevents us from pressuring our political leaders to build us the shelters that we desperately need.

Life *is* worth living. *The suicide syndrome is morally wrong.* Most of us really don't accept it, but when considering this one instance—nuclear war—we have been persuaded by our enemies to make an exception, and our own fears have multiplied this lie's influence. It has produced political paralysis that has led us to the brink of disaster as a nation.

A Stroll to Freedom

A very brilliant historian who grew up in Hungary tells the following story. His nation suffered the horrors of the Nazis from 1938 to 1945, and then it fell into the hands of the Communists.

He knows about tyranny.

He said that most people sat in their homes waiting for the new Communist government to take over. They hoped that they would be able to live in relative comfort, the way they had lived before the tyrants came. They were wrong. By the time they learned how wrong they had been, it was too late. It was a hard way to learn a biblical principle: if you try to hang on to some earthly thing for dear life, you will eventually find out how dear life really is. Jesus said:

> For whosoever will save his life shall lose it: and whosoever will lose his life for my sake shall find it (Matthew 16:25).

There was a way out for a brief period of time, but only a few people took it. It involved walking away from literally everything a person owned. If a person looked as though he intended to flee, he would never make it.

A man, his wife, and the children would set out for a stroll. They carried nothing, except perhaps a picnic basket. A suitcase would have been fatal to the plan, and possibly fatal to the people. The family's appearance indicated that they were going for an outing. The father might say hello in a friendly way to a policeman or some other official.

He would then buy a train ticket for the next town down the line toward the border. That raised no suspicions. At the next train station, he would get off, go to the window, and buy a train ticket for the next town, and so on, until they were two towns from the border. Then they would get off the train and do their best to walk to freedom across the countryside.

This escape method was limited to people who accurately assessed what was coming. They counted the cost and decided that it was better to leave everything behind. If they got across the border, they survived, at least for enough time to get across another border. But they could take nothing of value with them unless it could be easily concealed.

Most people didn't do it. They valued their immovable possessions too highly. Their possessions in effect owned them. They became the possessed. In some cases, their possessions cost them their lives.

They lost their freedom because they wouldn't pay the price when it was still available. They would not walk to freedom. The iron bars of totalitarianism closed in around them, their children, their grandchildren, and now their great-grandchildren.

The "good life" cost them their freedom, and it didn't last more than a few weeks or months after the political bars clanged shut.

Conclusion

The idea that life wouldn't be worth living after a nuclear attack is simply a call to stand in the front yard, eyes facing heaven, when the sirens sound.

If Americans really believed this myth, it would be one thing. But they really don't. It's a convenient way to say: "Don't disturb my illusions. I don't want to think about nuclear war. It won't happen."

But why is it a convenient way to say it? Because they have been brainwashed. It's easier to say, "I'd rather die than face a post-nuclear war world!" than it is to say, "It will never happen."

We look at the evidence, and if we're rational, we say to ourselves, "Not only could it happen, the Soviets and the Red Chinese have spent the equivalent of hundreds of billions of dollars on the assumption that it's *going* to happen!" It's easier to say the former because it has been drummed into our ears by thoughtless people who repeat a slogan.

That slogan is a crucially important component of Soviet psychological warfare. You should recognize it as such the next time it pops into your head.

12

SHELTERS AND
SOVIET TIMETABLES

There is one argument above all others that could block the construction of a shelter system for Americans. It is in the back of every strategist's mind, and in the stomachs of the decision-makers.

If we begin a crash program of building bomb shelters, will the Soviet Union launch a pre-emptive nuclear strike against us?

This single question is a major source of the political paralysis that keeps this nation at the mercy of the Soviet Union. This paralysis is giving them the time to build up their offensive forces, their defensive forces, and their system of allies.

It must be recognized that *this question has almost nothing to do with national defense*. There is no plan for our defense, except the now preposterous threat of our massive nuclear retaliation against a well-protected Soviet Union. We have no strategic defense — neither the off-the-shelf system of High Frontier (which could be deployed *now*) nor a high-tech laser system. There are no shelters for our people.

If the question has nothing to do with national defense, then what is it really all about? Simple. *This question concerns only the proper timing of surrender.* Moreover, appeasement is a policy that has, in the history of tyrannies, repeatedly *led to war* rather than deterred war. Soviet tyranny is no exception. The Soviets understand strength and have backed down repeatedly when faced with resolute and principled opposition. Into vacuums of weakness, however, they expand like a malignancy.

There is a feeling in high levels of our government that appeasement works. After all, we have been doing our best not to anger the Soviets for 25 years, and we have avoided nuclear war. This after-the-fact reasoning ignores the fact that for much of that time, we were actually stronger than the Soviets. It required over 30 years for the Soviets to build their overwhelming military machine and for appeasement in the United States to weaken us to our current position of danger. Appeasement hasn't worked. Only now are we beginning to actually use it from a position of weakness. If we do not immediately stop this policy and build a defense, then, in the words of Dr. Edward Teller, "We are lost."

Only in one sense is appeasement a defense-related question. It assumes that if we just stall, hoping for a way out, there will be some kind of unforseen event that will destroy the Soviet Union: a revolution, a plague, or an attack by China. In older days, we would have called such events "acts of God." We would have prayed to God for them. But today, our un-elected managers and experts are too sophisticated for all that, it seems. They agree with the Marxists: life is governed by historical forces, not a personal God. So we just have to be patient. Something will turn up.

It didn't turn up for Babylon the night the Medo-Persians invaded twenty-five hundred years ago (Daniel 5). It didn't turn up for Carthage when they voluntarily disarmed themselves at the insistence of Rome two thousand years ago. It didn't turn up for the Aztecs in Mexico or the Incas in Peru over four hundred years ago. Sometimes there are no more rabbits in a civilization's hat.

So we face a dilemma. Do we take steps now to reduce our total vulnerability in the long run, but risk total annihilation in the short run? Do we continue to submit to the Soviet Union's implied and explicit demand that we remain as hostages to their generals? Do we "play the China card" and try to get China to attack the Soviet Union? Or do we just sit tight, hoping that nothing bad will happen, and pretend that the Soviets aren't deploying their fifth generation of mobile nuclear missiles? Or do we make yet another American taxpayer-financed business deal? The great Russian writer Aleksandr Solzhenitsyn recounts a story of the early days of the Soviet Union. We really are not sure that it happened, but it is a common story, and most people who hear it instinctively believe that it could have happened.

I must say that Lenin foretold this whole process. Lenin, who spent most of his life in the West and not in Russia, who knew the West much better than Russia, always wrote and said that the western capitalists would do anything to strengthen the economy of the USSR. They will compete against each other to sell us goods cheaper and sell them quicker, so that the Soviets will buy from one rather than the other. He said: They will bring it themselves without thinking about their future. And, in a difficult moment, at a party meeting in Moscow, he said: "Comrades, don't panic, when things go hard for us, we will give a rope to the bourgeoisie, and the bourgeoisie will hang itself."

Then Karl Radek, whom you may never have heard of, who was a very resourceful wit, said: "Vladimir Ilyich, but where are we going to get enough rope to hang the whole bourgeoisie?"

Lenin effortlessly replied: "They'll supply us with it."[1]

Lenin forgot only to add: "With below-market loans, subsidized by their taxpayers."

The rope peddlers have dominated this nation's dealings with the Soviet Union for seven decades. Antony Sutton calls them the deaf mute blindmen.[2]

---

1. *Solzhenitsyn: The Voice of Freedom* (Washington, D.C.: AFL-CIO, 1975), pp. 5-6

2. Antony Sutton, *The Best Enemy Money Can Buy* (Billings, Montana: Liberty House, 1986).

Labor union officers know the story.[3] Political conservatives know it.[4] Historians know it.[5] Journalists know it. [6] Unfortunately, the voter's don't know it.

The Question of Courage

God told Joshua just before Joshua led the Israelites into battle for the promised land:

> There shall not any man be able to stand before thee all the days of thy life: as I was with Moses, so I will be with thee. I will not fail thee nor forsake thee. Be strong and of a good courage: for unto this people shalt thou divide for an inheritance the land, which I sware unto their fathers to give them. Only be thou strong and very courageous, that thou mayest observe to do according to all the law, which Moses my servant commanded thee: turn not from it to the right hand or to the left, that thou mayest prosper whithersoever thou go. This book of the law shall not depart out of thy mouth: but thou shalt meditate therein day and night, that thou mayest observe to do according to all that is written

---

3. Charles Levinson, *Vodka Cola* (London: Gordon & Cremonesi, 1978).

4. Larry Abraham, *Call It Conspiracy* (Seattle, Washington: Double A Publications, 1985).

5. Antony Sutton, *Western Technology and Soviet Economic Development*, 3 Volumes (Stanford, California: Hoover Institution, 1968-73).

6. Joseph Finder, *Red Carpet* (New York: Holt, Rinehart and Winston, 1983).

therein: for then thou shalt make thy way prosperous, and then thou shalt have good success. Have I not commanded thee? Be strong and of a good courage; be not afraid, neither be thou dismayed: for the Lord thy God is with thee whithersoever thou goest (Joshua 1:5-9).

We get the picture that God wanted Joshua to be strong and courageous. He said it three times.

We aren't invading a promised land. We also aren't using military force to gobble up anyone. Our inheritance is to be claimed by peaceful competition.[7] We are not military conquerors with a direct command from God. But we are supposed to pay attention to God's law. We are supposed to honor God by being God-fearing people who don't continually, defiantly violate God's ethical standards.

So we start with faith in God and confidence in His power. We demonstrate our faith and confidence by obeying Him. Any national defense system that is based only on a new gadget in the sky or a hole in the ground isn't going to work. It isn't even going to be tried. You want proof? Where is our civil defense program? Where are our anti-missile and anti-aircraft missiles? Where is our space-based defense? Where are our mobile missiles? Where are our cruise missiles — our 10,000 mass-produced, discount, one-megaton, slow, purely defensive, "call them back; we've made a mistake," and therefore "get the President's finger *off* the trigger" retaliatory cruise missiles?

---

7. Gary North, *Inherit the Earth* (Ft. Worth, Texas: Dominion Press, 1986).

They aren't there. Unless Americans start praying and demanding that Congress do something to defend us rather than threaten to throw a few obsolete missiles and airplanes at our enemies *after* they destroy us, we are headed for the worst disaster in American history. It may be the worst disaster since Noah's flood—and at least the good guys got themselves a shelter before that remarkable event.

We don't have shelters, but we do have a prayer.

Making a Deal With God

It's time for self-examination. Pretend we have shelters. Imagine that you hear the sirens wailing. An attack is coming. You may have only 15 minutes to grab your children and maybe a few personal items and make a run to the nearby shelter. You thank God and Congress for the shelter. You don't worry too much about its lack of comfort. The alternative is death. You don't get too fussy.

You are in the shelter. The kids are crying. They're scared. You're scared. It's crowded. It's like a subway. They tighten the blast doors. You wait.

What do you think about? All the good old days? Or the hardships to come if the bombs explode? The possibility of a ground-burst explosion that ends your life? What?

Wives worry about absent husbands. Husbands worry about absent wives and children. Everyone worries about the shaking of the earth. And everyone mentally begins to bargain with God.

All right, *start bargaining*. We mean it. We are deadly serious. Just start making a deal with God, right where you sit reading this book. God bargains, you know. He bargained with Abraham for the city of Sodom (Genesis 18). Moses bargained with Him for the people of Israel when God wanted to kill them. (See the next chapter: "The Desperation Prayer.") But remember this: *God always expects us to keep our part of the bargain.*

What will you bargain with then? You're in a hole. If the bombs go off overhead, you will be there for days, maybe weeks. You will go outside to a flattened countryside. The peace-loving Soviets will have done their number on your nation and your neighborhood. You may not be comfortable again for years. You may even be facing Cubans and Russians armed with modern weapons and poison gas. You don't know what you'll have when you climb outside. Mainly, you'll have the clothes on your back and your kids. You'll also have your neighbors. And perhaps for the first time in all of your lives, you will *be* neighbors.

What do you trade for your life as you sit or stand in that hole in the ground? What do you offer God for your survival? The answer is simple: *the rest of your life.* You offer Him your lifetime, God-fearing, law-obeying service. It's all you've got in that shelter.

Guess what? *It's all you've got right now.* Do you think that God is impressed with your money? Where did you get your money? It was a gift from God. "But thou shalt remember the Lord thy God: for it is he who giveth thee power to get wealth . . ." (Deuteronomy 8:18). What God wants out of you is faithfulness:

He hath shewed thee, O man, what is good; and what doth the Lord require of thee, but to do justly, and to love mercy, and to walk humbly with thy God? (Micah 6:8).

This message from a prophet was simply a repetition of God's law:

And now, Israel, what doth the Lord thy God require of thee, but to fear the Lord thy God, to walk in all his ways, and to love him, and to serve the Lord thy God with all thy heart and with all thy soul, to keep the commandments of the Lord, and his statutes, which I command thee this day for thy good? (Deuteronomy 10:12-13).

The Apostle Paul writes in the New Testament: "I beseech [plead with] you therefore, brethren, by the mercies of God, that ye present your bodies a living sacrifice, holy, acceptable unto God, which is your reasonable service" (Romans 12:1).

Right now, you can make the same bargain, no matter where you are, whatever your situation is, or whatever crisis you face. You can make the bargain with God right now that you surely will make in that shelter. Even better, you will get many opportunities between now and a nuclear showdown to indicate to God that you really are serious about your bargain.

The people who run our nation think they can safely make deals with the Soviets. That's like making safe deals with the devil. Better for the people in the neighborhoods to make deals with God.

If enough people in the neighborhoods make deals with God, *and actually start to keep their end of the bargain*, we will get our shelters. We might even get a collapse of the Soviet Union. A premature collapse of the Soviet Union is a lot better for us than a premature strike by the Soviet Union.

Now, just because you're not in a shelter right now, you may think you're safe. If you do, you haven't read this book carefully. You will probably survive a nuclear attack in a shelter. You will almost certainly *not* survive a nuclear attack if you're not in a shelter.

You think you're safe. You're safe only to the extent that the Soviets decide today not to launch a safe, clean, low-risk first strike against us. Tomorrow, they believe, it will be an even safer, cleaner, and lower risk to launch one.

You're safe for as long as the Soviet Union's Communist Party and General Military Staff decide to allow you to be safe for one more day. America's $300 billion a year military bureaucracy has no defense for you, except a less and less credible threat of terrorizing Soviet citizens after you're dead. In short, the only reason why you're not dead or dying right now is because by the grace of God, by means of His restraining or confusing the Soviet "giants," you have been given another day of life.

Make a deal with God. Then keep it. And if you have trouble keeping it, read the third chapter of the Book of John in the New Testament. You will get help in keeping your vow.

Will the Soviets Attack Prematurely?

There are no guarantees that, if we begin a crash program in shelter building, we won't pressure the Soviets to speed up their plans for a full-scale nuclear war. But where are the guarantees that if we sit around doing nothing, they won't do it in three years? Where is the guarantee that we won't be gassed or sprayed with some incredibly dangerous biological weapon, fresh out of some Soviet laboratory? If we wait, who says things are going to get better? Will the Soviets be weaker after they get a new generation of missiles? Will they be merciful after they get a fully deployed anti-ballistic missile system? Will their leaders become decent once they have more shelters for themselves and their families, a mile beneath Moscow?

Who guarantees an "act of God" before the missiles head for our towns and yours? There is only one way we can legitimately hope for a so-called act of God. That way is for God to act. The real God, not some traditional expression, not some supposedly random event.

We can be safe without bomb shelters. God is our shelter. But we sure as blazes can't be safe without God or shelters. And if we get right with God, one sign of this will be our ability at last to get Congress to admit that we really do face a national crisis. If Congress plays around as if we were not facing literal destruction, then Congress has betrayed us into the hands of our enemies. And if ever God had earthly enemies, it is the church-persecuting monsters who run the Soviet Union. Congress had better start making deals with the voters rather than with the Communists. Congress had better start making deals with God and not Satan. When you make deals with the Soviet Union, you're making deals with Satan. It's time to stop making deals with Satan and his unholy, tyrannical followers.

Are we using strong language? Yes! Are we exaggerating the nuclear threat? No! But even if the threat were technologically imaginary, our leaders believe it, and our people are petrified because they don't know that there is a $300 solution.

The Soviets are playing a waiting game. They have a billion Chinese to contend with. They have made a huge investment in military equipment that inevitably grows old. Their economy is straining now; as they fall farther behind the West's high-technology economies. Their military technology will become obsolete. Their economy will not take the strain. In other words, they are faced with the grim military hardware dilemma: "Use it or lose it."

They have a growing Islamic population that wants out of the Soviet empire. They have a sagging economy. They don't like taking risks. A shelter system makes it harder for them to blackmail us, but they still can level our homes and buildings. That is a powerful threat. All the shelters can do is protect our lives; they can't protect our developed urban real estate.

If the Soviets start a nuclear war, they cannot be sure of the results. If they were absolutely sure of its positive outcome, they would have launched the attack by now. Starting a nuclear war isn't a zero-risk deal. It is becoming a lower and lower risk for them, if counting chariots were all there is to war, but it isn't zero-risk.

Covering Our Backsides

Three times a year, the Israelites were required by God to journey to Jerusalem to present sacrifices and worship Him in His special city. The whole countryside was deserted. During the feast of booths (tabernacles) wives and children journeyed with the men. Probably a few workers stayed behind on a rotating basis, but most people went to Jerusalem. During Passover and Pentecost, only men were required to go (Exodus 34:23).

Eventually, someone would have wondered: Who guards our homes while we're far away? Who guarantees their safety from invaders? There was an answer: God.

> For I will cast out the nations before thee, and enlarge thy borders: neither shall any man desire thy land, when thou shalt go up to appear before the Lord thy God thrice in the year (Exodus 34:24).

They had to have faith in God. At the very least, they had to fear Him more than they feared invaders or thieves. To go about their lives in a God-honoring manner, they had to leave their property behind. To keep their property and blessings, they had to obey God's commandments. They had to demonstrate their faith in Him by acting righteously and responsibly, even when it appeared quite risky.

Whom should we fear: God or men? Whom should we fear: God or bombs? Jesus said:

> And fear not them which kill the body, but are not able to kill the soul: but rather fear him who is able to destroy both soul and body in hell (Matthew 10:28).

That is the answer to those who say we should continue to go about life as if there were no threat, and also to those who say that to begin to remove ourselves from our present status as hostages might enrage the pharaohs of Russia. Moses and Aaron faced a similar criticism when they told Pharaoh to let the people go on a three days' journey to sacrifice to God. Pharaoh punished the people by making them work harder. So the elders came to Moses and Aaron.

> And they [the elders] said unto them [Moses and Aaron], The Lord look upon you, and judge; because ye have made our savor to be abhorred in the eyes of Pharaoh, and in the eyes of his servants, to put a sword in their hand to slay us (Exodus 5:21).

In short, "Lay off, you guys! You're getting us in trouble with our Egyptian masters." When you hear this argument, or any variation, you are hearing the complaints of slaves. The elders of Israel were agents of the Pharaoh. *They were spokesmen of perpetual tyranny.* They said, in effect, "Let's make a deal."

The Only Available Cover

There is no guarantee that they will attack if we start building shelters. There is no guarantee that they won't. But there is evidence that they won't if enough God-fearing people start reforming their lives fast enough. If God's people obey Him, they get protection.

> He shall cover thee with his feathers, and under his wings shalt thou trust: his truth shall be thy shield and buckler (Psalm 91:4).

This is the cover to run to. There isn't any other cover left. We have no defense against nuclear attack. We have no shelters. We have no strategic defense. We have been stripped naked militarily. There is only one shield left: God almighty.

We don't think the Soviet General Staff has worked God into its computerized war games. We don't think the U.S. General Staff has, either. But God is the most important factor of all.

"God Will Take Care of Me!"

There is an odd attitude that some Christians have. They hear about a threat to their lives, and they say, "I won't worry about it. God will take care of me." Have you ever heard that one? Then comes the crisis, and who is the first person knocking at the door of the neighbor who spent time and money preparing for the crisis? You guessed it.

Then what does he say? "You owe me help. God says you do. You can't throw me out into the cold.

And by the way, I've brought along my family." In other words, when he says, "God will take care of me," he's really saying, "I'm not interested enough to take specific actions that could help reduce my family's risk. However, if we get into a jam, you will take care of me!"

You can imagine how this person would have responded to Joseph in Egypt, when God told him that a great famine was coming. (Joseph's solution: store up 20 percent of the harvest in the seven good years, so there would be food in the seven bad years.) You can almost hear the complaining: "Look here, Joseph. I appreciate your concern and all that, but you're becoming a fanatic about this famine business. Can't you see how much grain we're getting this year? You're asking me to give up 20 percent of my crop. Don't you know that God will protect us? You need to live more by faith. Please, no more of this gloom and doom stuff."

And when the famine hit, he would have been the first one in line to get the government-supplied grain.

God does take care of His people. When they die, they go to be with Him forever. But God's care of His people doesn't always mean physical protection. He sent Israel away into captivity. Good people became slaves to invaders, right alongside the bad people.

From the early 300s, A.D., Constantinople was a Christian city. It was the capital of the Byzantine Empire, officially a Christian civilization. In 1453, the Turks captured the city, slew thousands of the inhabitants, and abolished both Byzantium and Christianity as the national religion. Christians became non-citizens. Did God take care of them? Spiritually, yes; but their descendents still remain in political bondage.

Armenia, which adopted Christianity as the national religion, suffered from invaders century after century. In 1916, their Turkish rulers marched them into the wilderness and systematically killed between 800,000 and two million of them. It was the first case of modern genocide.[8] Did God take care of His people? Spiritually, yes; but their descendents remain in political bondage.

A year later, in 1917, the Bolshevik Communists took over Russia. They began persecuting all religions. Christians and Jews are second-class citizens in the Soviet Union. Stalin killed more than 30 million of the Russian people—by terror, famine, slave labor camps, and execution.[9] Did God take care of His people? Spiritually, yes; but their descendents remain in political bondage.

So when someone casually responds to the frightening information in this book, "God will take care of me," you know he is just trying to avoid personal responsibility for his future. He expects *you* to do it for him. And he thinks he will never face political bondage, let alone a one-megaton bomb.

It goes beyond this, however. He doesn't under-

---

8. Dickran H. Boyajian, *Armenia: The Case for a Forgotten Genocide* (Westwood, New Jersey: Educational Book Crafters, 1972).

9. Robert Conquest, *The Great Terror: Stalin's Purge of the Thirties* (New York: Collier, [1968] 1973), p. 710.

stand the God he says he believes in. He refuses to admit that Jeremiah's Book of Lamentations has anything to do with God's people. "That's just a lot of Old Testament stuff," he thinks.

He also doesn't understand the history of the Christian church. Terrible crises come as judgments. When a third of Europe died with the bubonic plague in two years, 1348-50, Christians perished everywhere. There was no place to hide. It spread from Italy to distant Iceland in two years. The experience affected European thought and culture for two centuries. And it kept coming back each generation for three centuries, until in 1665 it struck London and terrified the nation. Only the great fire of London in 1666 ended it, for it burned out the rats that were carrying the fleas that carried the disease.

God certainly takes care of His people. But He doesn't give them life insurance policies. He doesn't tell them that they'll be sitting pretty from womb to tomb, no matter what they do for themselves. God's kingdom is a kingdom of responsible, faithful, obedient action.

The Bible reminds us that we are supposed to plan for the future. Proverbs 30:25 says: "The ants are a people not strong, yet they prepare their meat in summer." God doesn't take care of the ants whether or not they prepare food in the summer. His care for the creation is based on the laws He establishes for the creation. (The fungus-tending *ant* builds it home 10 to 20 feet below ground level with tunnels up to 50 feet long—an excellent blast shelter system, too.)

Paul wrote to his assistant Timothy: "But if any

[man] provide not for his own, and specially for those of his own house, he hath denied the faith, and is worse than an infidel" (I Timothy 5:8). In short, a man who knows what seems to be coming but who refuses to spend some time, effort, and money to take care of at least his own family, is not a faithful man. He is worse than an unbeliever.

Anyone who reads this book *and really believes its warning,* but who then shrugs his shoulders, and walks away from his personal political responsibility by saying, "God will take care of me," had better examine his own heart. The New Testament says he is worse than an infidel. It says he isn't a Christian. It's one thing not to believe the facts in this book; it's another thing entirely to believe them yet do nothing politically to solve the problem.

Conclusion

At Pearl Harbor, a chaplain supposedly grabbed a machine gun and started shooting at Japanese airplanes. He uttered the classic line: "Praise the Lord, and pass the ammunition." It became a popular wartime song. Its theology is sound. He didn't say "pass the ammunition" before he said "praise the Lord." And he didn't praise the Lord without asking for more ammunition. The same is true for shelters. Run for God's spiritual cover now, so that you'll be able to run for civil defense cover later.

Make a deal with God. Then do whatever you promise. Don't forget to write to your Congressman. And if he brushes you off with a vague and noncommittal form letter, take it with you into the voting booth next time; it will help you to remember.

13

THE DESPERATION PRAYER

We don't have any shelters, but we still have a prayer. And there is one prayer, above all others in the Bible, that is appropriate for this crisis. It is the prayer of Moses after the incident of the golden calf.

Most Americans know part of the story. Moses went up Mt. Sinai for 40 days to be in the presence of God. During that period, God inscribed the ten commandments on a pair of stones. Probably there were ten commandments on each stone: one copy for God and one copy for the people. Both tablets were to be placed in God's holy container, the Ark of the Covenant. The ten commandments specified the general terms of the covenant between God and Israel.

What is a covenant? It's a legal contract, yet more than a contract. It is a specially binding pact between people under God. A marriage vow is a covenant, at least the vow that prevails in churches and synagogues. God serves as the ultimate enforcer. He requires people to fulfill their vows to each other in three institutions: the church, the state, and the family. These are special institutions that God has established to provide order. They are monopolies.[1]

God established the terms of the covenant between the Israelites and Himself. It was a priestly bond (especially the first five commandments) and a kingly bond (the second five). We might divide these emphases between church and state today.

Moses came down from Mt. Sinai, and he found the people worshipping a false god. They were also committing the standard, run-of-the-mill sin that generally comes with idolatry: adultery. God was outraged. They had broken the covenant. Moses displayed his own anger by throwing down both tablets and breaking them, symbolizing the broken covenant, and also symbolizing what God does to people who break His covenant. In the Old Testament, breaking the king's treaty (covenant) brought the king's wrath. Today, the state also acts much the same way. Break the law and you pay the penalty. But this covenant was with God, and the penalty was death. So God told Moses that He intended to kill all of the people (except Joshua and Caleb, who had remained faithful) and then raise up a new people out of Moses' family.

> They have turned aside quickly out of the way which I have commanded them: they have made them[selves] a molten calf, and have

---

1. Gary North, *Unconditional Surrender: God's Program for Victory* (2nd ed.; Tyler, Texas: Geneva Divinity School Press, 1983), Part II.

worshipped it, and have sacrificed thereunto, and said, These be thy gods, O Israel, which have brought thee up out of the land of Egypt. And the Lord said unto Moses, I have seen this people, and behold, it is a stiffnecked people. Now therefore let me alone, that my wrath may wax hot against them, and that I may consume them: and I will make of thee a great nation (Exodus 32:8-10).

This was serious business. Nuclear war is nothing compared to this. Nuclear war destroys the body and knocks down buildings. The judgment of God is eternal. Was this to be the end of the dusty road for Israel?

Here was Moses, facing a catastrophe. He had gone through all kinds of trouble leading them out of slavery. He and his brother Aaron had confronted the rulers of Egypt to their faces. The people had gone through punishments and trials. They were ex-slaves, and they were scared. They were also constant complainers. Now they had gone too far, and Moses knew it. What could he say to change God's mind?

The Prayer of Moses

What he said constitutes the single most effective prayer in the Bible. It was instantly answered. It allowed the Israelites to escape certain doom. It persuaded God to change His mind. (We don't want to go into a detailed theological debate about how we can say that God changed His mind. He was waiting to see what Moses would say. Would Moses say the right thing? He did, and God didn't destroy the Israelites.)

Moses did the wisest thing anyone can do when facing an outraged God who is about to bring judgment on someone who fully deserves everything he is about to get. *He appealed to God's own reputation.*

> And Moses besought the Lord his God, and said, Lord, why doth thy wrath wax hot against thy people, which thou hast brought forth out of the land of Egypt with great power, and with a mighty hand? Wherefore should the Egyptians speak, and say, For mischief did he bring them out, to slay them in the mountains, and to consume them from the face of the earth? Turn from thy fierce wrath, and repent of (turn away from) this evil against thy people. Remember Abraham, Isaac, and Israel [Jacob], thy servants, to whom thou swarest by thine own self, and saidst unto them, I will multiply your seed as the stars of heaven, and all this land that I have spoken of will I give unto your seed, and they shall inherit it forever (Exodus 32:11-13).

About 40 years later, just before the next generation was to enter Canaan and begin the military conquest, Moses spoke to them. He recounted this confrontation with God. Here is how he summarized his key argument:

> Remember thy servants, Abraham, Isaac,

and Jacob; look not unto the stubbornness of this people, nor to their wickedness, nor to their sin: lest the land whence thou broughtest us out say, Because the Lord was not able to bring them into the land which he promised them, and because he hated them, he hath brought them out to slay them in the wilderness (Deuteronomy 9:27).

You can see exactly what Moses was doing. He was reminding God of His promises—His covenantal guarantees—to Abraham, Isaac, and Jacob that God had made centuries earlier. He was saying, in effect: "Is God a liar? Is He a covenant-breaker? Far be it from anyone's mouth, O God! Destroy them, and your enemies will call you a liar."

"So let these bums off the hook."

"The Egyptians and their self-proclaimed god, the Pharaoh, know that you said that you would deliver these people from slavery. You defeated them in Egypt. You brought the ten plagues on them. You led the Israelites through the Red Sea. You smashed that God-hating empire in front of the whole world. You now say that you will destroy these, your people? If you do, those same lying pagans, those same God-despising tyrants, those same God-cursing rebels will tell anyone within earshot that you're some impotent, two-bit God who couldn't deliver on your promises."

"So let these bums off the hook."

So what did God do? He let the bums off the hook.

Bums on a Nuclear Hook

God is not happy with what this nation has become. We abort our children. We ignore God seven days a week. We fail to check out the textbooks our children are assigned at school. We tax our neighbors in order to benefit our own special interests. And we do it all in the name of compassion, charity, and the American way. (If you don't think this list is valid, then make up a list of your own. The point is, we all know that a long, long list could be put together. It wouldn't take much work to do it.)

The Puritans and other Protestant Englishmen who came to North America in the 1600s established a series of civil (government) covenants with each other under God. Other Christian groups that came here in the next century generally accepted the terms of these various covenants. People agreed to honor God's law. The Bible was the law of the land in the colonies. The state constitutions reflected this. The U.S. Constitution shows biblical influence. If it had been a radical break, it would never have been ratified by the people who had ratified the various state constitutions.

All of this is to say that *this nation is under the terms of God's covenant.* It is an ethical covenant. Over and over, God told His people that if they broke the terms of the covenant, they could expect judgments —specifically, war (invasion), plagues, and famine.

A lot of you may scoff at such a view of U.S. history. It is the same sort of scoffing that went on in intellectually sophisticated circles just before the French Revolution and the Russian Revolution.

When the sirens sound, people will no longer scoff. God isn't dead. Most of us will be after a first strike.

Patrick Henry's famous "give me liberty or give me death" speech of 1775, delivered in St. John's Church before the Virginia Assembly, contained the words, "Peace, peace—but there is no peace." He was quoting the Bible: Ezekiel 13:10 and Jeremiah 6:14. In both cases, the prophets were predicting the coming judgment of God against Israel. Ezekiel used the analogy of a nation that had thought itself protected by a weak wall; that wall would surely fall, he warned them. God Himself would knock it down (Ezekiel 13:13-15).

Peace comes through people's faithfulness to God, God's law, and to each other. It doesn't come through military strength alone. Patrick Henry knew that in 1775. Our leaders seem to have forgotten it today. If men would read the Book of Deuteronomy, chapter 28, they would have a better idea of how we get peace, and also how we lose it. It is not strictly a matter of military hardware. A successful military defense system must be supported by the faith of a people.

We have broken every law in the moral book. We think we have God's favor because a long time ago we went to church, or did a good deed, or won a war for democracy. The moral account book is overdrawn.

In the spring of 1980, Admiral Jeremiah Denton was running for the U.S. Senate from the state of Alabama. Admiral Denton had been a Navy pilot, and his plane had been shot down. He was a prisoner of war in North Vietnam for seven years. His book, *When Hell Was in Session*, was widely distributed nationally, and it was made into a T.V. movie starring Hal Holbrook.

A political meeting was held at the Capitol Hill Club in Washington. A young political hot shot came into the room and announced: "Do you know what that idiot Denton just said? He was asked, 'What is the most serious national security problem in the United States?' and he answered, 'Premarital sex.'"

Retired General Al Knight was in the room. Gen. Knight is also an ordained Episcopal priest. "He's right," Knight said to the hot shot.

Denton was close. Maybe there are other sins that are worse, but he was on the right track. A nation that condones open sin, or whose leaders stand by impotently while sin runs rampant, is going to have internal security problems. They are nothing compared to the *external* security problems.

Mercy for Sinners

There are people who apparently believe that God just wouldn't let the Soviets launch a nuclear attack against the United States. They talk as though God has some sort of unwritten rule that He will never, ever bring a nation under judgment.

What happened to Israel? Read the Book of Lamentations by Jeremiah to discover just how God deals with national rebellion. But there is one fact to bear in mind: there are two kinds of judgment.

There is judgment unto *restoration* and judgment unto *oblivion*. God always judges His people in the first way.

The problem arises when His people have become some other god's people. Is the true God really finished with them? Does He ever really finish with them? We had better hope not.

Remember, too, that God no longer deals with only one society as His exclusive people. If it takes a nuclear attack on the United States to call Christians around the world to repentance and a renewed faithfulness, what is that to God? Are Americans so special that God just can't get along without us? The Book of Job (chapters 38-42) has the answer. It is not a comforting answer to those who believe that "God just wouldn't let that happen to America."

Nevertheless, there is that original covenant. We are still known as a Christian nation (which indicates what a mess other formerly Christian nations are in). We do send out more missionaries and print more Bibles than any other nation on earth. Our special position presents God with a problem. Remind Him of His problem. Say a prayer something like this:

What will the nations say, O God, that have tried to elevate themselves above your very throne? What will they say if a God-hating society run by murderers and thieves obliterates this nation from the face of the earth—literally? What if they who have said, "There is no God," succeed in destroying the remnants of a once-faithful nation? And what if they destroy that nation at the very time that a new attitude and a new heart become part of a growing number of people? Will you leave a testimony to all mankind that you tolerate evil for decades, and when your people at last begin to repent and make restitution, *then* you bring judgment? What will faithful men think, and what will your enemies say? How will this magnify the name of the Lord?

When we start praying prayers like this one, morning and evening, then maybe God will start taking us seriously, and we will get our shelters, and get an anti-missile defense. Maybe then we will get a stay of execution.

If we get no shelters, the Soviets could blow down most of the buildings in the country, and kill 200 million people. The whole operation would take about 30 minutes.

Soviet power is awesome. It reminds us of the Bible's account of the last battle between God and Satan. They possess power as men that can be compared only with the power of God in judgment. And that is why they can be taken down. That is why they *will* be taken down.

The question is: Before or after we get shelters?

Sleepwalkers Anonymous

Perhaps the most successful rehabilitation program ever discovered is Alcoholics Anonymous. Men and women who have become addicted to alcohol, and who have been incapable of breaking this addiction by themselves, become sober. They usually stay sober for life — for *dear* life. How do they do it?

At every AA meeting, when someone stands before the group to offer his story, he begins, "I'm Bill D. I'm an alcoholic." (No last names are used publicly.) He makes a public admission of his affliction every time he speaks at an AA meeting. He thereby reminds himself of his weakness, and he shows others that the first step to sobriety is to admit what you have become: addicted.

There are twelve steps that the AA member is expected to take. The authors of this book, while not alcoholics or former alcoholics, are so impressed with these twelve steps, and so impressed with the tremendous success of the program, that we reproduce them here. We think that every American should adopt this set of twelve principles of action, no matter what crisis we face, any time we face one . . . especially the present military crisis. Just substitute your perceived crisis for "alcohol."

We admitted that we were powerless over alcohol — that our lives had become unmanageable.

Came to believe that a Power greater than ourselves could restore us to sanity.

Made a decision to turn our will and our lives over to the care of God as we understood Him.

Made a searching and fearless moral inventory of ourselves.

Admitted to God, to ourselves, and to other human beings, the exact nature of our wrongs.

Were entirely ready to have God remove all these defects of character.

Humbly asked Him to remove our shortcomings.

Made a list of all persons we had harmed, and became willing to make amends to them all.

Made direct amends to such people wherever possible, except when to do so would injure them or others.

Continued to take personal inventory and when we were wrong promptly admitted it.

Sought through prayer and meditation to improve our conscious contact with God as we understood Him, praying only for knowledge of His will for us and the power to carry it out.

Having had a spiritual awakening as the result of these steps, we tried to carry this message to alcoholics, and to practice these principles in all our affairs.

In an astounding percentage of cases, the alcoholics who follow this program are then delivered. No other program matches it.[2]

---

2. For the story of AA, see *Alcoholics Anonymous* (3rd ed., 1976). It is published by Alcoholics Anonymous World Services, P.O. Box 459, Grand Central Station, New York, NY 10163. For the twelve steps, see the book, *Twelve Steps and Twelve Traditions* (1952), also published by AA.

We can think of no better example or model of what the people of this nation need to do in order to stop sleepwalking into a nuclear nightmare without civil defense. We wish the President and the Supreme Court would make such a public statement. We wish Congress would. But if they don't, then we are going to have to do it for them. They have done nothing effective to reduce our risk of getting nuked.

Conclusion

Shelters are important. Prayer is vital. We can survive without shelters, though not if the Soviets at last decide to strike. Shelters will reduce our risk, strategically speaking. Prayer will reduce our risk, judgmentally speaking. But it would be better to have prayers *and* shelters. An anti-missile system would be nice, too. But we have to begin with something. That something isn't shelters. It isn't a political pressure campaign to get shelters. The first item on the agenda is prayer. That's all we have left.

God owes us nothing except His judgment. But He doesn't owe the Soviets anything, either. God owes Himself honor. He owes His name glory. Let's pray that He gets what He wants by judging the Soviets rather than us.

We have included two psalms in the back of this book, Psalm 83 (a prayer of God's judgment) and Psalm 91 (a prayer of man's dependence). Both prayers are important. Both prayers have a place in public worship.

By God's grace, let us pray our public prayers in church rather than in shelters. And also by God's grace, let us have shelters for praying, too . . . just in case.

CONCLUSION

Our conclusions are unpleasant. We live in a world which is fundamentally unpleasant, but superficially pleasant. We live in a high-technology, high-risk dream world. American voters think of this nation's problems as if we were viewing a pre-television Saturday morning serial at the movies. Those of us who are over age 40 remember. At the end of each weekly segment the hero faces certain death, and the screen announces: "Continued Next Week." But next week, he escapes. Always. And in the final week's chapter, he wins.

This isn't the sort of world we live in today. There are unhappy endings. The heroes don't always survive. Ask a surviving Cambodian, if you can locate one. Go see "The Killing Fields" if you can't locate one. Or read *The Murder of a Gentle Land*. It looks as though it will be our turn soon. Our country is fast approaching a tragedy — a thermonuclear tragedy.

We live in a world which is tottering. It rests on shaky foundations, and these foundations are, above all, moral in nature. To return to a nice, pleasant, stable world, we need to rebuild the foundations. Nothing less than this will get us out of the mess we are certainly in. Star Wars' high technology alone won't save us. Neither will low-technology holes in the ground. National repentance alone offers us security. Neither chariots nor holes in the ground are sufficient.

This isn't to say that we don't need the technologies. We *do* need the technologies. God usually operates in history through normal, everyday means. He isn't performing miracles on the evening news broadcasts three nights a week. But if His people really need a miracle, *and they ask for one*, He very often gives them one. Not always, however; there are no guaranteed free lunches in God's kingdom. There are times when He allows His people to face the consequences. The Book of Lamentations *is* in the Bible, after all. The Armenians *were* slaughtered by the Turks.

It seems doubtful that we can expect Congress to vote for the technologies that will give us a fighting chance, unless we first pray the kinds of prayers that God responds to with His favor. Prayers come first. Congress comes second, if Congress will come at all. Better to trust in the sovereign power of God than to trust in the good sense of Congress. For thirty years, Congress has voted for thousands of programs that have done little more than run up a two-trillion-dollar national debt and waste trillions in all the taxes they cost. And we still don't have the holes in the ground that could save our children's lives or our own.

God's people today are sleepwalking. They aren't being defended, and they don't know it. They need the defense technologies, but they don't know it. So they need a miracle, but they don't know that, either. They go about their daily activities as if they weren't in mortal danger. They *are* in mortal danger. *You* are in mortal danger. This danger is increasing daily.

We have not written a book to promote despair. It does no good to write despairing books. We have written a book that offers a ray of hope in a world where the evidence points to despair. The evidence is clear. The evidence is so clear that only a member of Congress could be blind enough (or overwhelmed enough with legislative trivialities and re-election campaign details) to ignore it. You now know what the evidence is. *The evidence says we now face surrender to the worst tyranny in man's history or annihilation by that enemy.* But there is such a thing as faith. There is legitimate hope.

What is faith? "Now faith is the substance of things hoped for, the evidence of things not seen" (Hebrews 11:1). Elisha's servant despaired because of the large army of Syrians that faced them. "Alas, my master! How shall we do?" Elisha's reply is still valid today:

> And he answered, Fear not: for they that be with us are more than they that be with them. And Elisha prayed, and said, Lord, I pray thee, open his eyes, that he may see. And the Lord opened the eyes of the young man; and he saw: and, behold, the mountain was full of

horses and chariots of fire round about Elisha
(II Kings 6:16-17).

The chariots of fire are with us still, or the technological equivalent of modern chariots. The problem is not chariots. The problem is the spiritual rebellion that has led God to bring enemy chariots to
the very gates of the city. The weapons of destruction
that face the West are simply a *sign* of the problem,
not the problem itself.

If we despair because we don't have enough
chariots, then we have misunderstood the problem.
Until about 1975, we had more chariots than the
enemy. The problem from 1917 to 1975 wasn't the
West's lack of chariots. The problem was the West's
lack of humility before the God who has given the
West its strength. He has now raised up the worst
bunch of thieves and criminals in history to remind
us of the magnitude of His blessings and the magnitude of our ungratefulness.

Don't worry about those who can kill the body
but not the soul. Fear Him who can destroy the body
and the soul.

Our problem isn't technology; our problem is a
lack of humility before God. The solution to the
problem isn't more weapons than the Soviets have.
We cannot possibly catch up with them in weapons.
They are too far ahead. We need *defense*, not more
nuclear weapons. We need to stop thinking in terms
of MAD, with its evil doctrine of retaliation against
other civilians. We need to target their leaders, their
military installations, and their ships. We also need

to target their accomplices in Cuba. We need to target their missiles—not on the ground, where we can't get them, but in the stratosphere, after the war has begun. Initially and primarily, we need to get out of the line of fire. We need holes in the ground.

But all of this is just more war games activity. What is needed is something more important than war games strategy. The ultimate solution is faith in God coupled with the will to resist. The will to resist is based on the long-term *will to victory*. It is that spirit that says, "I shall not die, but live, and declare the works of the Lord" (Psalm 118:17).

What to Do in a Flood?

There is the story of the Christian who was caught in a flood. The water kept getting higher around his house, so he climbed onto the roof. He prayed, "Lord, deliver me from this flood." A man in a motorboat came by. He asked the Christian if he wanted a lift. "No, the Lord is with me," he replied.

The water rose higher. "A test of my faith," he thought to himself. Another man in a motorboat came by. "Do you want a lift?" he shouted? "No, the Lord is with me." He stayed on the roof as an act of faith.

The water was now over the edges of the roof. But a helicopter appeared overhead. "We'll throw you a rope," the bullhorn sounded. "No, thanks, brother; the Lord is with me," the man on the roof shouted back, and waved the helicopter on.

The water rose, washed the man away, and he drowned. At the gates of heaven, an angel met him.

The man was shocked. "Why has this happened to me? I exercised faith in Almighty God!"

"What did you expect?" the angel replied. "We sent you two motorboats and a helicopter. What did you want, a miracle?"

God sent two motorboats and a helicopter, but the man ignored the gifts. God tells us the obvious by means of our own eyes: we need shelters to preserve our lives. The Swiss listen. What do Americans do? Americans put their fingers in their ears, shut their eyes tightly, and keep telling themselves, "God will take care of us." That's what the Israelites told Jeremiah, too, just before the Babylonians broke through the walls of Jerusalem.

What would you pay for a hole in the ground the day the sirens sound? Everything you own. But if there are no holes in the ground for us to climb into, will the bureaucrats even bother to sound the sirens? Will they even give us an opportunity to prepare to meet our Maker and say goodbye to our children, this side of death?

If we voters and taxpayers aren't willing to spend $300 a child to save their lives, then why should we expect the military bureaucrats to admit publicly their failure to defend us? Why should we expect them to sound the sirens to let us say goodbye to the children we voters were too cheap to protect?

It is one thing not to tell very young children about the danger, though the authors of this book have told our older ones what they can expect. It is something worse not to tell the voters what they can expect. The United States government since the death of President Kennedy has lied to us by remaining silent in the midst of a terrible danger. We voters had better not lie to ourselves any longer.

Prepare to meet your Maker every day. Don't expect sirens to warn you of this meeting—a meeting that the Soviet high command may have scheduled 25 minutes from now. They will have the technical power to schedule that meeting for you until Congress wakes up and builds us those shelters.

To admit the need for civil defense shelters, many government officials must implicitly admit that they have been derelict in their duty to us in the past. Do you really expect our elected representatives to admit this unless we openly threaten them with defeat at the next election?

Send Your Congressman a Message

You have to tell Congress to defend us. If you won't do this, why would you expect anyone else to do it? You have to write your Congressman a letter. You have to send him a telegram. If you won't do this, why would you expect anyone else to do it?

If necessary, phone his local district office, or phone him in Washington. Ask the girl who answers the telephone for the Congressman or for the name of the Congressman's Administrative Assistant. Write the assistant's name on a sheet of paper, and then ask to speak to him. Then tell him that you would like him to tell the Congressman that you think he should vote for a nuclear shelter program as soon as possible.

Why the Administrative Assistant (or AA)? *The*

Administrative Assistant is the man who tells the Congressman what the voters in his district are demanding. Get the attention of the Congressman's Administrative Assistant, and you have put your cause at the top of the pile. Just tell the Administrative Assistant politely that you want protection for your family, and you expect the Congressman to vote for a program that will get the shelters built immediately. Don't argue about it. Don't be impolite. Don't try to convince him of anything except your personal concern.

Here is the key: you *must* insist on a *written reply* from the Congressman. Give your name and address to the Administrative Assistant. Ask him to bring this up with the Congressman, and ask the Congressman to send you a written reply.

If enough of you call him, you will get a clear reply. If not many of you call, he will mumble, just as those who preceded him have mumbled on the civil defense question for thirty years.

You can call Congress (House or Senate) simply by dialing this number, and asking for your Congressman's office:

(202) 224-3121

Most of all, *you have to remember during the next election how he voted on civil defense shelters.* He has to believe that you won't forget what he failed to do. Keep in mind the words of the late Senator Everett Dirksen concerning the motivation of all elected representatives:

"When we feel the heat, we see the light!"

There are a few Congressmen who have taken a principled stand for the defense of the people of the United States. They are, however, a small minority. We need to help these few men by bringing pressure to bear upon their colleagues. It is our responsibility as voters who are legally in charge of the country to make them feel the heat.

If you won't do this, why would you expect anyone else to do it?

Pray and Pay

Don't expect somebody else to do your work for you. That's why we're facing a crisis: for forty years, voters have expected their representatives to do the right thing, on time, inexpensively, even when there was nobody pressuring them to do it. This expectation has proved false. That isn't the way Congress works. Congress responds to direct political pressure from people who the Congressmen believe can make them or break them. Silent people who trust their Congressmen can't break them and won't make them, so such people can safely be ignored, the Congressman thinks. He is probably correct. Conclusion:

Either we pressure Congress, or the Soviets will pressure us — at 200 pounds per square inch of pressure.

If you aren't willing to scream and yell and keep the pressure on your Congressman and Senators until at least your children or grandchildren have shelters (even if you presently think that *you* can't bear to face life on the far side of a nuclear attack), then don't expect God to perform a miracle to bail us out. Tell your Congressman you want the children of this nation to stop serving as hostages. *Tell him you're willing to pay.*

If you aren't willing to pay for the shelters, then don't expect a miracle from God.

Even more important: if we don't *pray* for Congress, as well as threaten politely any member of Congress who fails to vote for a civil defense shelter system, then we deserve to die as surely as a generation of Congressmen, Senators, and Secretaries of Defense deserve to die with us. Tom Lehrer's humorous song of the 1960s isn't funny any more: "We will all go together when we go."

If you accept their assurances that everything is just fine, then you may die before you can change your mind. We are not exaggerating. We all could die before the next election. Just 25 minutes after the Soviet generals press the buttons, we *will* die. Once the missiles fly, all we've got is a prayer. Better to pray now, and then have shelters *and* a prayer.

Best of all, better to pray now, have all of the shelters completely installed, continue to pray after they're built, and thereby send the Soviets a clear message that *we have the will to resist*. If we do this, the missiles probably won't fly.

Power Religion versus Dominion Religion

From the beginning, evil men have put their faith in power. The exercise of power is their answer to the crises and problems of this world.

Power religion is a fraud. Kingdoms rise and fall. Tyrants rise and die. But the power religion always fails. The Soviets will choke if they try to swallow the world. They will fail. The problem is, they may remove the United States from the map before they fail.

We are coming to a great confrontation in history. The most powerful example of the power religion in the history of the world is stumbling to its demise, but it is stumbling like a mad elephant, crushing everything in its path. We see a war between good and evil; as always, it is also a war between the kingdom principle and the empire principle. The kingdom is a decentralized social order that operates from the bottom up, with men responsible ultimately to God. The empire is a centralized order that operates from the top down, with men responsible primarily to the State. The principle of power leads to the attempt to establish an empire. The Soviet Union is simply the latest manifestation of the principle of power. It is a revival of ancient Egypt.

Moses confronted Pharaoh in Egypt. We must do the same.

The Responsibility of Pastors

The prophets were always in conflict with the court prophets who told the kings of Israel and Judah that everything was just fine, that God was on their side, and that they would win every battle. The court prophets were liars—unreliable, lying, taxpayer-financed court prophets. (A good example in the Bible is I Kings, chapter 22.)

It was the unpleasant task of God's prophets to prophesy unpleasant events to kings. The prophets were persecuted for it. The people didn't want to hear the bad news; neither did the judges, court prophets, and kings.

The prophets prophesied unpleasant events because they understood the relationship between rebellion against God and the external, visible, unpleasant judgments of God. These judgments weren't simply internal, psychological judgments; they were visible for all the world to see.

The mark of a prophet is his willingness and ability to make good judgments. He can prophesy "peace, peace," when there are moral grounds for expecting God's external blessings on society. Some of these blessings are listed in Deuteronomy 28:1-14. On the other hand, he is equally willing and able to preach "war, war," when there are moral grounds for expecting God's external judgments. Some of these are listed in the much longer section of Deuteronomy 28:15-68. There are far more curses than blessings listed in this section of the Bible.

When pastors are silent in the face of imminent external national judgment, they have in principle gone over to the side of the court prophets. It is convenient to remain silent. It is unpleasant to become a troublemaker. The evil king Ahab confronted the prophet Elijah with these words: "Art thou he that troubleth Israel?" (I Kings 18:17).

And he [Elijah] answered, I have not troubled Israel: but thou, and thy father's house, in that ye have forsaken the commandments of the Lord, and thou hast followed Baalim (verse 18).

The essence of following false gods (Baalim) is to abandon God's law. It is the job of the true prophet, in contrast to the huge number of false court prophets, to call people back to faith in God and to obedience to God's law.

Any pastor who is not doing both — preaching both *faith* and *obedience* — is an implicit court prophet. Remember Admiral Denton's words when he was running for a U.S. Senate seat (which he won). He was asked what the nation's most important national security problem was, and he answered: "Premarital sex." Such a "strange" response might have lost him the election. He didn't care. It is time for pastors to be equally outspoken.

Our problem isn't a lack of hardware. Our problem is a lack of faith in God, as revealed by our lack of obedience to God's laws. We will learn how costly such rebellion is. The modern-day version of the Assyrians or Babylonians — the Soviet Union — may soon teach us a lesson the world will never forget. If they do, we will not be around to remember the lesson.

If the pastors won't bring this message to their congregations, then why should they expect this problem to go away? The court prophets died with the kings they served. Better to be fired by a hostile congregation of sleepwalkers. Pastors should keep in mind the verse in Psalms that President Kennedy quoted to end his last written speech: ". . . except the Lord keep the city, the watchman waketh but in vain" (Psalm 127:1). If the churches are silent, the end is near — not the end of *the* world, but the end of *our* world.

We have included two Psalms at the back of this book for use in public worship in churches. We strongly suggest that pastors tell their congregations what the problem is, and that they lead their congregations in public prayer on a regular basis with our mortal enemies as the target. The Soviets since 1917 have repeatedly declared war on God, the West, and this nation. We had better call the God of heaven to stand at our side in this crisis.

Without God at our side, holes in the ground won't help very much. Without a determined, principled resistance to Congressional paralysis, Congress won't build us the holes. Without the holes, this country can't offer a principled resistance to the Soviet Union. Without principled resistance to the Soviet Union, this nation cannot long maintain its independence — and maybe not even its existence.

You have heard the story. What are you going to do to help?

But be ye doers of the word, and not hearers only, deceiving your own selves. For if any be a hearer of the word, and not a doer, he is like unto a man beholding his natural face in a glass [mirror]: For he beholdeth himself, and goeth his way, and straightway forgetteth what manner of man he was. But whoso looketh into the perfect law of liberty, and continueth there-

in, he being not a forgetful hearer, but a doer of
the work, this man shall be blessed in his deed
(James 1:22-25).

APPENDIXES

Appendix 1

SHELTER OPTIONS FOR NON-OPTIONAL SHELTERS

The Chinese system of tunnels is the best shelter system on earth. City-dwelling Chinese citizens can move immediately into a completely protected environment from their homes, work, or other locations. Then they simply walk out of the danger area — walk with complete protection. If fallout is severe, they remain in the tunnels or migrate through them to a safe area. Moreover, if they were to suffer an invasion, their tunnel system would serve as an invaluable defense system against Soviet ground forces — the same kind of tunnel-based military system that the Communists used so effectively in Vietnam.

This tunnel shelter system demonstrates that the Chinese have the will to defend their homes, families, and country. Their defensive preparations for survival are sufficient in and of themselves to deter Soviet aggression. Even in their largest city, they can be 30 feet underground in seven minutes, and then simply walk to safety. No "subway car" crowding for two weeks, no danger of insufficient warning to reach shelter, and a place to sleep at night during the period of rebuilding above ground. They only lose their buildings, not their lives.

Then why don't we propose tunnels? In our proposed system, you jump into a safe hole, but you can't walk away and hide in the countryside for several weeks. You may have to stay in that crowded, unpleasant hole for weeks, right under the rubble.

The reason why we propose a second-best system is cost. If our government thought enough of us to spend an amount comparable to the per capita expenditures of the Swiss—an amount about equal to the U.S. military budget (we shouldn't call it a defense budget, since it just isn't defending us) for a single year—then we, too, could have a tunnel system. We could then allow private businesses, if they wished, to fill the tunnels with shopping malls, schools, hospitals and other facilities for which we can always use extra space. Think of the savings in cooling and heating expenses! They would pay rent for the privilege, of course. Maybe the rent income could be used to repay some of the national debt.

The Chinese, of course, did not spend $1000 per person. Instead, they spent large amounts of individual labor. Americans can afford machines, and they prefer to use machines. We can't afford to give our labor. Besides, we aren't used to hard physical labor.

Why not build a tunnel system with machines? This is an excellent option, but the problem is motivation. The Chinese leaders *did not lie to their people* about the very real Soviet threat, or about their inability to cope with that threat in the absence of shelters. Also, of course, in the Chinese totalitarian system, when the leaders say dig, you dig!

In the case of the United States, most engineers and scientists have proposed modular, non-tunnel systems simply because they are cheaper. However, since our leaders have not been truthful with the American people about the danger, and also about the potential of blast shelters to eliminate that danger, even these less expensive systems have not been deployed.

In preparing this book, we considered numerous shelter options and considered the current political climate. (Future political climates aren't very relevant, since without shelters, we are less likely to be able to participate in the future, at least not as decision-makers.) We decided to propose the very best modular type protection, and to reduce cost by crowding and discomfort rather than by increased risk. In that way, we are able to propose an excellent system based on $200 per person for the blast and fallout shelter, plus an additional $100 per person for food, tools, and other items to aid in survival and reconstruction after an attack. Crowding could be eliminated for an additional $50 per person. These low prices also depend upon relatively large 150-person shelters and savings from mass production and procurement during a large building program. You can't have one installed in your back yard for five people at those prices per person.

The important points are: 1) the danger is immediate; 2) our government is not acting to meet that danger; 3) the simplest and most effective steps *must* be taken *now*. The simplest and most effective first step is a high-quality blast shelter system for our entire population, *deployed immediately*.

Maybe the government will decide that we are worth more than $300 each but less than the $1000 required for a tunnel system. Maybe the government will decide that we are worth less than $300 but more than zero. What then?

For about $1000 per person, we could build luxurious, low-occupancy shelters of the modular type. "Spend World War Three in a Winnebago, not a subway car!" This would be foolish. That much money would buy a tunnel system.

For $700 per person ($600 for the shelter and $100 for post-attack food, tools, and supplies) we could build excellent blast shelters according to current, standardized and fully effective designs with an occupancy rate of about 10 square feet and 100 cubic feet per person and with very comfortable accommodations. They would be similar to the design proposed herein, except that there would be a lot more space per person—either more shelters or bigger ones. They would also have more amenities. Of course the size of shelter units is somewhat arbitrary. It is affected largely by the problems of mass production and installation of very large shelters and the inefficiencies of very small ones.

Also, some localities have unique solutions available. The underground caverns in Kansas City, the deep subways of the nation's capital, and the mine tunnels of the Pacific Northwest can all be utilized instead of the standardized shelters. However, New Orleans, because of the high water table, would require more expensive shelters. Incorporation of these kinds of alternatives into the system would provide better shelters at comparable cost in a few localities. Overall, however, the cost of the entire United States shelter system would be about the same per person.

How much money can be saved if we keep the shelter quality high in terms of safety but lower it in terms of comfort by putting more people in the same shelters? Minor changes must be made to allow for increased ventilation, water storage, and furniture, but these don't change the cost much. New York subway cars are designed for 2.3 square feet and 20.8 cubic feet per person. World War II German bunkers for civil defense were designed for 2.1 square feet and about 20 cubic feet per person. The adult human body occupies about 2.3 cubic feet, so about 12 percent of the available volume is filled in a 20 cubic foot system.

During attacks the German bunkers were sometimes occupied at triple the design occupancy or more, but only for relatively short periods. Successful American tests have demonstrated relative comfort at about 4 square feet per person and the Swedish official shelter recommendation is for 5.4 square feet per person. The Soviet standard is 5 square feet. The seating area of economy class on a Boeing 747 is about 4.5 square feet. (These occupancies are calculated by comfortable researchers in peacetime.)

With nuclear explosions going off, a person's options become limited, rather like the options of the Germans who overcrowded the bunkers during the Hamburg firestorm raids. They had severe discomfort during the raids, but crowding saved many extra lives. They left those crowded bunkers and rebuilt 80 percent of the industrial productivity of Hamburg within 5 months.

It should also be kept in mind that not all of the shelters will be in high fallout areas, and fewer still will be in areas where the destruction of aboveground, fallout-safe structures is complete. The shelter's water and food provisions for each individual will be stored in convenient, easily carried small containers, so that each person will be able to leave the shelter immediately after the attack if fallout conditions allow it. They can move to some other less crowded location, if one is available.

With our people in blast shelters, and therefore with a lower incentive for the Soviets to attack our civilian areas, we expect that many people will need the blast shelters for only a short time. Of course, everyone must be in them initially, because we can't know before the attack where the weapons will be detonated. Shelters must all be supplied for full occupancy for the full two weeks if that proves to be necessary. If some localities did not have blast shelters, that fact alone would invite direct attack on those localities.

The point is, severe crowding in the shelters is better than no shelters at all. For this reason, the $200 system is proposed in this book and used as an example in this book. This is an austere, crowded, but very high-protection system. It would cost the American people $47 billion, plus another $23 billion in food and recovery provisions. This amounts to 3 percent of the federal government's usual expenditures for two years. (Actually, it would be less than $23 billion, because the federal government has already bought some of the food through various farm subsidy programs. *That food is already being stored at taxpayers' expense.* Payment by citizens for the post-attack food storage program would be partially indirect: higher future farm prices, since the current farm commodity surplus would be taken permanently off the market.)

If our representatives in Congress decide that we deserve more space per occupant, they can vote to build additional shelters. That way, we don't mess up production schedules. We just get more of the same. In short, "Buy two; they're small."

The entire system can be *completed* in less than two years by means of existing industrial facilities, and with existing and currently underutilized industrial capabilites in steel and concrete production, metal-forming, and earthmoving. The currently idle American assembly line facilities can be used to produce the habitability items, such as radiation meters, hammock beds and chairs, water storage containers, ventilation equipment, and blast valves.

But what if Congress only spends $100 per person? We cannot go to 1 square foot per person. Alternative approaches include: 1) shelter for the women and children, but not the men; 2) shelters for the "important people" and not the rest of us; 3) shelters without survival equipment: you can't stay inside long, and everybody brings a box lunch.

The bottom line is that we must start building modular shelters for the children now. Surely we can agree that we have no moral right to leave them unprotected. Then we build for our soldiers, then for our homes and businesses. If we like the results, we just keep right on building. Maybe we'll even build so many that there will be comfortably low occupancies. Maybe we'll even tie them together with tunnels. Maybe our children, our grandchildren, and our civilization will have a future after all.

Appendix 2

SHELTER LOCATIONS

We must be certain that the shelters will be located so that most of them cannot be destroyed even by the worst possible deliberate attack on the shelters themselves. *This is the best way to ensure that such an attack will never take place*. We must place the shelters according to Soviet *capability*, not according to our perceptions of their intentions.

The United States (not including Alaska) contains approximately 3 million square miles. Nuclear explosions of 500 to 1000 kilotons (1 megaton) at optimum height can destroy most buildings over a 50 to 100 square mile area. Therefore, with an attack by 10,000 explosions, the Soviets could destroy the buildings in an area of about 1 million square miles. Excluding, therefore, buildings in desert, forest, and very rural areas, they have the capability of destroying most of the buildings in the United States.

As their nuclear arsenal grows, and as the number of their "delivery vehicles" grows, they will be able to knock down even more of our buildings.

In practice, of course, they will concentrate explosions in urban areas and around military installations, and keep weapons in reserve for threatening other countries into submission. Such threats will be very effective in a world in which the United States no longer exists. Even so, *it is unlikely that any city or large town will be free from a direct attack.* Clearly we cannot defend our buildings. Only an anti-missile defense system can do that—a *deployed* strategic defense, *not* a research and development program.

An air-burst attack on our buildings will not harm our people if they are in properly designed, 200 psi sure-safe blast shelters. The blast shelters could only be harmed by a ground-burst attack. Besides being much less effective at destroying buildings, a ground-burst attack would also not be effective in destroying very many of our shelters.

A ground surface burst, 500- to 1000-kiloton explosion produces a crater about 0.03 square miles in area. You read it correctly: three one-hundredths of a square mile. This can vary, of course, in accordance with soil type and other factors. In addition, soil and rock ejected from the crater covers an additional 0.1 square miles to a significant depth—a depth that, in the absence of a tunnel system, might fatally trap the occupants of an underground blast shelter. In addition, there is severe ground-transmitted shock and pressure in the immediate vicinity of a nuclear explosion. For these reasons, it is impractical to build civilian blast shelters that can resist ground bursts within their own 0.6 square mile location. Six-tenths of a square mile isn't much area.

The shelters described herein would be sure-safe outside of a 0.6 square mile area around a ground burst explosion of a one-megaton nuclear weapon. They would be surely destroyed within a 0.3 square mile area. In between, they would be partially destroyed.

What if the Soviets, knowing that we are going to be in our shelters, simply targeted the shelters with ground bursts? For 230 million people, we will need 1.5 million shelters, as compared with 10,000 Soviet weapons. Clearly they cannot kill many of us unless we put the shelters too close together.

Half of the people of the United States live at a density of 1,500 people per square mile or less. They would need less than one shelter per 0.1 square miles. The low densities of people in rural locations would require a few more minutes on average to reach shelter, or else placement of extra shelters with fewer people per shelter. In the worst case, therefore, the Soviets could only endanger six shelters per explosion and could only surely destroy less than three with one bomb.

An additional 30% of our people live at densities of more than 1,500 but less than 6,000 per square mile. For them the risk would be a minimum of 3 shelters per explosion and a maximum of 24.

When these facts and also the circumstances of those people living at even higher densities are taken into consideration, we estimate that *a maximum of less than 10 percent of our blast shelters could be destroyed by an all-out ground-burst attack on the shelters themselves with the entire Soviet nuclear weapons inventory.*

This damage does not compensate for the larger disadvantages of neglecting to destroy our buildings and military installations in order to concentrate on our civilian shelters. Fewer buildings would be destroyed, because ground-burst explosions are much less effective for blast damage than air-burst weapons. The buildings near the explosion are destroyed, but the land surface area covered by destructive blast forces is much less. In summary, if we had large numbers of small blast shelters distributed at our *non-evacuated* population density, the casualty rate would be so low as to render an attack on the shelters impractical and ineffective.

We need the blast shelters so that we can be sheltered near our usual locations. We will not need to evacuate. But blast shelters are a little more costly than simple fallout shelters. Why not evacuate into the countryside and build fallout shelters?

The Soviet civil defense systems relied in part upon evacuation during the years that their blast shelter system was being built. Of course, they had the advantage of warning, since it is their military doctrines that call for a surprise first-strike. Ours do not.

Now that the Soviets have completed a formidable blast shelter system, they no longer depend upon evacuation. Unfortunately, some of our planners still propose evacuation schemes that assume long warning times. They assume that we will see the Soviet evacuation and then have time to act. Evacuation is no longer required by the Soviets. This was an obvious development, since their military strategy of a surprise first-strike could hardly include the obvious warning of evacuation.

In the face of the Soviet threat, the Chinese built an evacuation system — 30 feet underground. The Chinese plans do not depend on warning and evacuation time. They know their enemy. In addition to their early knowledge, the Soviets have the following advantages: we have fewer attack weapons; most of those weapons will be destroyed by the Soviet's first strike; those that we manage to launch will encounter their formidable strategic missile defense systems; and, finally, if any do get through, they will not do much damage to a country that has protected most of its industry and has blast sheltered its population.

Shelter density is illustrated by reference to maps 1 and 2 in this appendix which are outline maps of Washington, D.C. and its surrounding counties: Montgomery and Prince George's (Maryland) and Fairfax (Virginia); and maps of Los Angeles and Orange Counties in California.

In 1980, Washington, D.C., Montgomery County, Fairfax County, and Prince George's County had populations of 638,400, 579,100, 596,900, and 665,100 respectively, for a total of 2,479,500, or about 1% of the US population. The corresponding surface areas are 63, 495, 393, and 487 square miles respectively. Therefore, the average population densities in these four regions are 10,100, 1,700, 1,500, and 1,400 persons per square mile.

Because most people within the three counties are concentrated in about one half of the areas, the actual density is about 3000 persons per square mile, with densities approaching twice that, or 6000 per square mile, in a few localities. In Washington, D.C. itself, the additional increase in density involves a little higher risk per shelter.

In order to kill everyone in the shelters, an area of about 700 square miles would need to be attacked with about 2000 ground-burst explosions, on one city, Washington, D.C. and its suburbs, in order to kill 1% of our people. Those 2000 weapons represent 20 percent of the available Soviet arsenal. On the other hand, only 10 to 15 explosions in the air would destroy the buildings in this entire area, and would also kill nearly all of the people who were not inside shelters (shelters that do not now exist).

Los Angeles County and Orange County had, in 1980, populations of 7,477,400 and 1,932,900, and areas of 4,070 and 798 square miles respectively. The corresponding densities are 1,800 and 2,400 persons per square mile. These people are, for the most part, concentrated in one-half of Los Angeles County and two-thirds of Orange County, so that the effective density is about 4000 persons per square mile in a 2,500 square mile region that contains 4% of the United States population.

Would the Soviets deliver 60 percent of their entire nuclear arsenal on these two counties alone, just to kill all of these people in their shelters? Or would they prefer to use only about one percent of their weapons on these two counties, in order to destroy most of the buildings and kill those people who are not in shelters? We think the answer is obvious. The shelters will survive.

These examples are applicable to most of the United States. Most of us live in areas like these, or in areas where the population density is lower, and which would be therefore even more safe from Soviet attack *if* we had blast shelters available.

One notable exception: New York City—Manhattan Island, Brooklyn, Bronx, and Queens—contains 6,700,000 people living at densities of 64,900, 31,900, 27,800, and 17,500 persons per square mile respectively. The area is only 242 square miles. These people could be killed by 500 Soviet nuclear weapons even if they were in the proposed shelters. As improbable as this may seem to us, it is unwise to trust so many lives to the rationality of an evil and irrational opponent. The obvious solution is to build better, deeper shelters and perhaps even tunnels in New York and its suburbs. There are very few equally heavy population densities in the United States, so they do not markedly change the overall program, even if special provisions must be made for them.

These high population centers are also the most vulnerable to the possibility of a single nuclear explosion (probably ground burst) by terrorists. Potential immediate civilian casualties from such an explosion could be hundreds of thousands, with over a million killed by fallout. However, with shelters and with just 15 minutes' warning (perhaps from a ransom demand), the immediate casualties could be reduced to a few thousand. Fallout casualties, even with no warning from the terrorists, would be completely eliminated. People would enter the shelters when they heard the explosion or were alerted by the authorities.

The high-quality blast protection of properly designed shelters limits the killing radius of nuclear weapons to such a great extent that it would be impossible for the Soviets, even with their huge first-strike genocidal weapons inventory, to kill more than 10 percent of the American people if they were in those shelters, and the shelters were installed at our current living density. This fact is not compromised by the very high shelter occupancy rates which we recommend herein, in order to bring the overall cost within currently realistic boundaries. After a minimum number of shelters are installed, guaranteeing that our children can survive, and our soldiers and we ourselves can survive, we can always install more shelters to lower the occupancy and increase our comfort.

Map 1

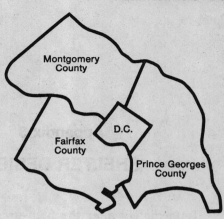

Map 2

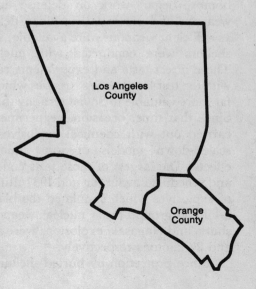

Appendix 3

SHELTER DESIGN

Immediately after the first atomic bombs were exploded over Japan in 1945, scientists in the United States, including many who had helped build the bombs, began work on defense against nuclear weapons and particularly civilian defense. As soon as sufficient weapons were available, various tests of shelters were conducted with nuclear weapons. These direct tests and experiments came to an end with the test-ban treaties, treaties which have proved far more valuable to Soviet tyranny than to freedom. Since that time, occasional experiments have been carried out with chemical explosives that provide scaled-down models of some nuclear weapons effects. The largest of those tests conducted in 1985 and scheduled again for mid-1987 utilized 4 kilotons of explosives which simulated the blast wave of an 8-kiloton ground-burst nuclear weapon. The Hiroshima and Nagasaki explosions were air bursts of 12 and 22 kilotons respectively.

Since protection by buried shelters proved relatively simple, most research since the 1950s has been directed at the problem of reducing cost through engineering innovations. There was an especially large amount of this research carried out in the early 1960s at President Kennedy's order. He ordered this work preparatory to building a national shelter system. This system, which was abandoned after his death, is needed far more urgently today than it was in 1961 when Kennedy concluded that it should be built. If the American people remain unsheltered and therefore perish, Kennedy's murder in Dallas will prove to be an historical event which led step by step to the destruction of the free world.

There are several thousand research reports and primary scientific articles which are relevant to blast shelter protection from nuclear weapons. In February 1986, the Emergency Technology Library at Oak Ridge National Laboratory contained a subsection of about 1,000 of these. These 1,000 articles formed most of the primary research material from which we have selected a single standardized shelter design for this book. This design is quite similar to a standardized design which is under development by the scientists at Oak Ridge and to designs which have been repeatedly proposed by engineers and scientists over the past 30 years.

The Earth-Arching Phenomenon

When a steel tank, much like a large fuel tank or a large road culvert with sealed ends, is buried under sufficient granular soil and subjected to the high pressures of a nuclear explosion, the sides of the tank yield slightly, and the earth compresses to form a *protective arch over the tank*. The tank must be *strong* and *flexible*. In this way, the strength of reenforced concrete can be duplicated by a low-cost, lightweight structure. Since *the soil also provides an inexpensive massive radiation shield*, this is an ideal solution to low-cost blast and radiation protection.

In order for earth arching to protect the tank from the blast, the tank must not be buried below the water table. There are several means of avoiding this problem in locations where the water table cannot be avoided. One simple method is to install the tank as usual, and surround it with reenforced concrete to provide the extra strength required.

The shelter discussed herein is a tank made of ¼ inch thick steel. The tank is 11 and one half feet in diameter and 40 feet long. It is small enough to be transported by truck to the desired location. 75 percent of the tank is designated for living space and 25 percent for storage and common apparatus and facilities.

Table 1 in this appendix summarizes the cost of a blast shelter based on such a tank, and Table 2 summarizes the space for each occupant. These tanks would need to be buried with about 10 feet of soil over the top. Tank shelters of this size can be entirely manufactured and equipped in existing metal-fabricating shops and delivered on trucks in complete, functional condition to the installation sites.

An earth moving machine, usually either a large backhoe or a medium size dragline, digs the hole and lowers the shelter into it. The entryways are then either bolted or welded on, and the dirt is replaced. In some cases, where the dirt is poorly suited to earth arching, road gravel would be used as back fill instead of the original soil.

Entry to the shelter is from each end through tubular entries designed with two right-angle turns that will decrease reflected radiation entry. See Figure 1 in this appendix for an illustration. One entry is vertical with a ladder. The other is angled with a slide for rapid entry. This entry works like the tubular fire escapes that were popular in multiple story public schools in the past, or like an airline escape slide. The two entries give safety in case one should be plugged with rubble, and the slide entry allows for very rapid entrance in case of emergency.

These entries also serve as ventilation shafts through smaller tubes that join them and connect with the ground surface. The ventilation shafts have blast valves that close automatically when hit by bomb blast waves. The entries themselves have steel blast doors which are locked mechanically after the people have entered. These parts of the shelter are designed for maximum simplicity as is most of the other shelter equipment. It is important to understand that nuclear explosions are hard on shelters. If some part won't work after it is banged around, bent out of shape, and generally mistreated, then you don't want it on your shelter.

Nuclear explosion blast is an especially impressive phenomenon. Imagine a force that can actually compress the surface of the ground by as much as a foot. The blast doors are flush with the ground to avoid reflected pressure and flying objects. They are backed by large concrete collars which transfer the blast load to the ground rather than to the shelter where it could crush or bend the steel shell.

Once inside the shelter, air for breathing, water for drinking, and a mechanism for cooling to remove metabolic heat (especially in a crowded shelter or a warm climate) are the most immediate needs.

Ventilation and Cooling

Air can be supplied from outside air with special precautions to avoid contamination with fallout, chemical, or biological warfare agents. Each shelter is therefore equipped with two air passages, dust filters (in the entryways where the accumulation of some fallout radiation will not harm shelter occupants), and specialized filters to remove dangerous chemical and biological agents. These filters are delicate, so blast valves are installed to protect the filters.

As a backup to this system, and also for use during periods of very high external danger, such as during the attack itself, each shelter contains stored oxygen and carbon dioxide-removal chemicals sufficient to supply the occupants for two days. This means that the shelter can be closed completely if necessary. Test equipment for monitoring oxygen, carbon dioxide, carbon monoxide, temperature, and absolute pressure levels is also provided. Additional days of air supply can be provided at a cost of about $12 per person per day.

The best supply of safe water is from a well. This is the source which was utilized in most German bunkers. A well is also required under Soviet shelters. With a well, water is plentiful for personal hygiene as well as simple drinking requirements. Manual pumping must be available and is relatively easily accomplished.

As a backup in case the well is lost to ground motion or contamination, each shelter must store the drinking water required for life for all of the occupants for a period of two weeks. Excellent modular containers have been developed for this purpose. These have the advantage that they can be stacked in the entryways during long term occupancy in order to further reduce radiation levels.

Cooling is extremely important. Depending upon climate and time of year, these shelters could be occupied by 20 or so people whose metabolic heat can be removed by the walls and earth surrounding the shelter. If the shelter were not cooled, however, at the design occupancy of 150 persons, the occupants would eventually die from thermal effects and would be very uncomfortable within a short time.

This shelter, therefore has two entirely redundant cooling systems. This reduces risk to those inside. First, there is air cooling. Outside air is pumped through the filters and the shelter in much greater amounts than are needed for breathing. The air carries away metabolic heat. The air pumps are redundant, so that in the case of failure of the electricity, manual air pumps can be used.

After the attack, there would be no electricity other than battery power for lights, radios, and meters. Power could be supplied by an emergency generator, but we have not included a generator in this austere design. Bicycle-type air pumps where the wheels are actually fans have been developed for shelters. The shelter occupants would take turns peddling the pumps.

Second, there is water cooling. Shelter occupants would also take turns on the floor-mounted manual water pumps. The shelter well system is connected to copper cooling coils that cool the shelter with well water. Cooling with well water permits operation of the shelter in a completely closed configuration, and it also backs up the air cooling system.

With air, water, and cooling provided, and the survival of the occupants assured, the shelter then provides human comfort items.

Other Support Equipment

The toilets and sinks are built into the well water system which provides sewage removal and a surplus of water for hygiene. In case of loss of the well system, the toilets are provided with simple storage containers for waste.

A battery power system, recharged in peacetime from the electric utilities, runs lights and provides electricity for other purposes as is done in recreational vehicles. Batteries sufficient for radios and emergency lighting at low levels for long duration are provided. There are a few electronic items that need to be in each shelter in advance. Most important are dosimeters to measure the accumulated radiation dose of each occupant, and survey meters to measure the current radiation rate at any location. These will include external probes for measurements outside the shelter as well as inside of it.

In addition, each shelter will have several pocket-size, two-way, shortwave FM radios which allow communication between all shelters within a ten mile radius. These are portable for use outside after the attack as well. Radio receivers of the more usual kind will allow us to listen for information from greater distances.

The radios and meters need to be protected from EMP which could destroy their circuits. Since the shelters themselves are what scientists call Faraday cages, they provide electronic shielding that protects the equipment as long as it is not tied to an outside antenna or probe. The antenna or probe must be reconnected after the attack has ceased. Several FM radios would be present in each shelter for redundancy and for post-attack communications.

Since the shelter is cylindrical, a flat floor is installed. The space under the floor is used for storage. Furniture is among the items stored there. The shelter is furnished entirely with hammock type chairs and hammocks for sleeping. These hammocks are suspended from the ceiling by flexible cords. They are not installed until the shelter is actually occupied.

Cloth hammock furniture has several advantages. First, it is easily stored and inexpensive. Second, it is soft. If some people should lose their balance and fall, there will be no edges of fixed furniture to cause injuries. If nuclear weapons explode near the shelter, the suspension cords will absorb part of the shock of shelter motion. In addition, occupancy experiments have shown that hammock furniture is a space efficient means of providing comfort to shelter occupants.

Stored with the hammocks will be gas masks and protective clothing for use in case shelter occupants should need to leave the shelter for any reason. Fire extinguishers, hand tools, a cutting torch, and related items will be stored there too.

The shelter medical kit and emergency library is important. The medical kit will contain the usual first aid items and also some special items which should be used by trained physicians. If no physician is available, however, trained medics assigned to the shelters or even untrained individuals guided by the shelter library will be responsible for health care.

The medical kit will contain specific agents like atropine for treatment of chemical warfare victims and antibiotics for biological warfare victims and burn victims. Potassium iodide tablets to prevent thyroid damage from moderate radiation exposure will be included.

The shelter library would contain medical books, survival books, nutrition books, instruction books covering the various equipment and contingencies, and Bibles.

Each unoccupied shelter would be equipped with an electronic surveillance system, so that local police will be notified of intruders. This need arises because the shelters can never be locked. In case of emergency, we cannot permit delays that might be associated with unlocking shelters. The surveillance system will deter vandals and notify the authorities about any intrusion which may have caused damage. Penalties for vandalizing shelters or stealing equipment from them must be very tough. Such crimes threaten the survival of the country.

Maintenance vans that test the shelter's various systems and assure that all is in good order will visit each shelter routinely at 18 month intervals. This continuing maintenance will cost about $2 per person sheltered per year. The surveillance system will require about $1 per person sheltered per year for monitoring cost. Overall, we estimate that the maintenance, monitoring, and repair costs of the nationwide shelter system would be about $5 per person sheltered per year.

The Soviets have a large branch of their military with the sole job of providing civil defense — as do the Swiss. In the Soviet case, 100,000 full-time professionals are supplemented by millions of civil defense reservists and a national requirement that everyone, even grade school children, receive extensive civil defense instruction every year.

These large personnel commitments are very valuable, as are the facilities provided — facilities that cost two to ten times more than those that we are suggesting here. In the American shelters, it will be crowded, it will be uncomfortable, and, without a large standing army of civil defense professionals, it will also be amateur night — but we'll survive.

Actually, when the shelters are installed, the local communities should organize their use. Community disaster relief organizations do not need to be provided by the federal government. Nuclear war, however, requires the initial special technology that Congress must provide. Give the American people blast shelters, and they'll read the instruction books themselves.

Table 1
General Cost of 150 Person Shelter

Item	Dollar Cost (1986)
Cylindrical room 11 feet, 6 inches × 40 feet (steel and concrete)	8,500
Entryways, doors, ventilation tubes	4,000
Excavation and installation	2,000
48 hour internal air system	4,000
Water cooling system	2,500
Well	4,000
Toilets (2) and sanitation	1,000
Hammocks, fans, lights, batteries, post-attack library, comfort items, medical and emergency equipment	3,000
	29,000

Table 2
Occupancy by 150 People

Item	Provision
Cross-sectional area per person	2.3 square feet*
Volume per person	20.7 cubic feet*
Cooling per person	800 BTU/hour
Oxygen per person	1 cubic foot/hour
Carbon dioxide removal	1 cubic foot/hour
Toilets per person	1 for 75 people
Capital cost per person	$193
Maintenance cost per person/year	$5**

*This is based on 75% of the available tank area and volume. The adequacy of these parameters is based on design and occupancy from historical examples of war shelter and marine and ground transport. Obviously, more room per person would be desirable and could be provided at increased cost by adding extra shelters close by. To save life, however, crowding is acceptable. These values could be doubled without extra shelters at an additional cost of $50 per person by increasing the room size.

**Based on travelling vans that exercise all systems in each module once every 18 months.

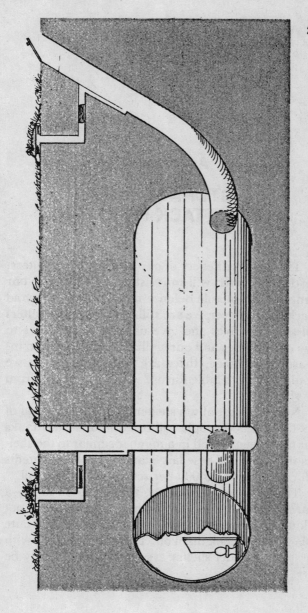

Figure 1

Appendix 4

STORAGE FOR
POST-ATTACK RECOVERY

The deterrent effect of our prayers, our shelters, our demonstrated will to resist, and (hopefully) our eventual anti-missile defense may allow us to avoid attack. If, however, we are still attacked, our shelters will save our lives and give us a fighting chance to save our families and our civilization. In order to increase this chance, there are some things that we should have available for use when we emerge from the shelters.

Near each set of ten shelters that house a total of 10×150 or 1,500 people will be additional steel tanks that have been buried in a manner similar to the shelters themselves. These large tanks and their contents will cost about $150,000 per set to buy and install.

The primary item in the tanks will be food—a year's supply of food for each person. We are not talking about freeze-dried camping rations and cute little stoves to cook them on. Those things come with the luxury model shelter system. They will only be available if our government decides that we are each worth as much as a Swiss or a Russian or a Chinese citizen. (That means that *we voters* must decide that we're worth that much, and we then must convey our estimate to our elected representatives in Washington.)

These tanks will contain bulk grain, beans, and corn right out of the farm bins and grain elevators in the United States. These items in combination with some other essentials such as vegetable oil, salt, and essential nutrient supplements will keep us alive and well-fed for a full year. There are ways of preparing such rations that are palatable and nutritious — in fact some health food advocates eat this way voluntarily.

In most regions, with the lives of the people saved, normal food supplies will begin to be restored in far less than a year. However, to make certain that everyone will be well-fed, regardless of the damage and restoration time of our food production, storage, and transportation systems, we must have plenty of stored food available. After all, we sold (translation: "gave away at low-interest loans") the Soviets the grain that they needed for *their* civil defense storage supplies. Why shouldn't we do the same for ourselves? The required grain, beans, and corn are already available in our government-financed farm surplus storage programs.

An ex-convict named Joseph convinced Egypt's Pharaoh of the wisdom of such a food storage program. Why can't American voters convince their representatives of such wisdom?

In addition to food, this storage module will contain medical supplies and equipment for use by professional physicians. Medicines which can only be produced by high technology will have a high priority here.

Tools will be next. The emphasis will be on agricultural and carpentry tools, and on tools required for the repair of industrial machinery. These will be primarily hand tools and simple items that will aid in the bootstrap procedure of restoring our productive economy.

The rubble will contain a great amount of partially damaged and undamaged items that we can use to rebuild. Except in areas of high density frame construction, much of this rubble will be untouched by fire and will be of substantial value.

Seeds will also be stored in this module. The food storage itself will provide seeds for mass production of staples and the addition of non-hybrid seeds will serve as insurance of that. (Crops grown from hybrid seeds do not produce seeds for the next planting that can produce a high-quality crop. They are one-shot, one-planting, high-yield seeds. There may be no hybrid seed producers around to produce seeds for the post-attack crop.) In addition, we need vegetable seeds, and the means to reestablish our agriculture on a local level. In time, this local food production will be replaced by the restoration of our farms and distribution economy, but each group of shelters should have the ability to provide for itself in the meantime.

In addition, the tank will contain individual face

masks with filters and protective clothing to resist
chemical and biological warfare agents and test kits
to identify these risks. These are in addition to those
in the primary shelters themselves.

Finally, this tank will contain those items and instruction materials necessary to recharge and repair
the primary shelters, so that we can be ready in case
we are attacked again with weapons of mass destruction.

It is true that we could rebuild from the rubble
alone; that we could forage for food in the rubble
and participate in heroic scenarios to transport food
from wrecked storage facilities; and that we could
rebuild our industry from the tools available in areas
that are not bombed and from facilities that have
been hardened to protect tools from damage.
Uniform success at these efforts throughout our
damaged country without substantial suffering and
loss of life is unlikely, however, unless we store post-
attack supplies near our shelters.

These facilities will allow us to rebuild much
more quickly and to be strong enough to continue
our defense. Therefore, we should choose to spend
the additional $100 on post attack provisions rather
than upon additional comfort during the relatively
short stay in the shelters.

Appendix 5

RADIATION AND FALLOUT

Nuclear radiation is always with us. Low levels of radiation are contained in the air we breathe, the walls and floors of our houses, most of the things we use, and the substances of which our own bodies are constructed. Most of this radiation comes from the disintegration of unstable atomic nuclei or from radiation that hits the earth from outer space, cosmic radiation.

The most penetrating radiation is called gamma radiation. It, along with the less penetrating alpha and beta radiation, bombards our bodies continuously.

Every minute approximately 7000 particles of background radiation penetrate the average person's body. Of those, about 4000 particles of radiation hit the person's tissues and do damage, while about 3000 go on through without impact. In addition, about 40 atoms within the body itself decay every minute. Their radiation damages the tissues in which they are contained.

Some activities increase our exposure. For example, the radiation at high altitude in a passenger airplane is about 40 times as great as at sea level, or about *300,000 particles per minute per person.*

This radiation is as natural to our environment as sunlight or rain. Our bodies have mechanisms to repair the damage, and, in some ways, the background nuclear radiation may actually help to improve our health.

If, however, nuclear radiation hits us in much greater quantities than are usual (heavy fallout from a nuclear weapon could increase the dose rate by 10 million-fold or more), our bodies' repair mechanisms can be overwhelmed so severely that we become ill and may even die.

Our bodies can continuously tolerate without illness about 10,000 times the normal background dose. We can tolerate 50,000 times the normal dose for a one-week period, providing our bodies have ample opportunity for several weeks of rest and repair before such a dosage is repeated. About 15 percent of the damage is repaired per week. We can even tolerate 10,000,000 (ten million) times the normal background dose for a one- or two-hour period. This dose would, however, use up all of our radiation tolerance for the next several weeks.

The unstable atoms in fallout that produce high radiation levels do so because they decay *very rapidly.* They decay so rapidly that, *within two weeks*, the number of these atoms and the radiation which they produce is *1,000 times less* than it was one hour after the nuclear explosion which produced the unstable atoms.

Clearly, if we just keep away from this radiation for a while, the passage of time eliminates its threat. By putting distance and the mass of a radiation barrier like dirt or concrete between ourselves and the radiation, we become safe from harm.

Most explosions in a nuclear war will probably be air bursts. In air bursts, the nuclear fireball does not touch the ground. These, like the air-burst explosions at Hiroshima and Nagasaki, will not produce fallout. Some explosions, however, would occur on or near the ground. The dust, dirt, and rock sucked up by these explosions would become radioactive, drift with the wind, and settle down upon the countryside.

Some places would have none of this fallout, and some others would have so little that it would pose no threat to health or life. In other places, however, the fallout would be so extensive that people would need to stay sheltered until its radiation decays.

This means that some people would need to spend part of each day in shelter; some would need continuous shelter for a few days and then shelter part of each day after that; and, in the worst case, some people would need continuous shelter for up to two weeks.

Shelter from fallout would often be available outside of the blast shelters themselves. In case it isn't available, or if it has been destroyed by the blast, each shelter must have life-support capability for all of its occupants for a two-week period.

Some people try to guess where the bombs will fall and which ones will be ground-bursts. In this way, they try to lower shelter costs by providing shelter based upon their own theoretical estimates or war games. This is a very dangerous procedure. *Every American deserves and must have protection from the worst possible Soviet attack.* We cannot predict what the detailed plan of their attack would be—especially after they have observed our preparations.

If we all have two-week blast and radiation shelters, then in all probability, most of us would not need to stay in the shelters for two weeks. If, of course, we don't have the shelters, then our enemies can design their attack to easily kill most of us.

Protection from nuclear radiation is as simple and straightforward as protection from normal sunburn by means of shade. Our "umbrellas" just have to be thicker. The peculiar properties of nuclear radiation require only that the shading elements be several feet thick.

Protection from nuclear explosion blast is as straightforward as protection from air-blast by the windshield of your car (which causes an effective wind velocity of 50 to 60 miles per hour). The enormous energy of the nuclear explosion blast requires, however, a much stronger windshield.

In order to scare the American people into inaction, and in order to promote certain special interest political causes, many false statements have been made about the effects of low doses of nuclear radiation. It is claimed, for instance, that legions of genetically ruined children will be born, and that radiation will cause tens of millions of new cases of cancer. These statements are unprincipled and untrue.

Even in a worst-case, all-out nuclear war, nuclear radiation would harm primarily those individuals whose exposure exceeded their bodies' short-term repair capabilities.

The increased low levels of radiation to which survivors of the first few weeks would be exposed would do long-term harm to some people. That harm would, however, affect such a low percentage of people that it would be largely unnoticed.

It is absolutely essential that each American know the truth. They have been told *lies*. Lies like "nuclear winter" and "legions of mutant children from increased background radiation" have helped to make us defenseless against Soviet tyranny. War is horrible, but nuclear war will be much more horrible if we fail to prepare for it. Falsehoods about radiation that paralyze us with fear, and thereby diminish our preparations, are dangerous. That is why the Soviets have a small army of propaganda experts whose job it is to spread fear and disinformation around the world. Sadly, too many well-meaning and intelligent people, even scientists who have not specialized in radiation's biological effects, have become accomplices of these Soviet disinformation specialists. They have been duped.

To be free from tyranny we must be free of misconceptions, especially misconceptions that have been deliberately spread by people who do not want this nation defended from Soviet attack. We must know the truth about our enemies and also about the technology with which they threaten us.

Then said Jesus to those Jews which believed on him, If ye continue in my word, then are ye my disciples indeed; and ye shall know the truth, and the truth shall make you free" (John 8:31-32).

Appendix 6

SELF-PROTECTION
AND EXPEDIENT SHELTER

The *facts* are clear:

1. The nuclear threat to each individual American is immediate and severe.
2. Protection from this threat can be provided by known techniques.

In view of these facts, there are two rational positions: a call for immediate national civil defense and strategic defense deployment, or a call for individually financed self-protection and expedient shelter. These are respectively the optimistic and the pessimistic positions.

We are optimistic. We believe that, through the enlightenment of our people and the intervention of God, our nation's voters can be convinced to get the government to provide their defense. With that defense, we will deter nuclear war. We may even prevent it. If not, at least our civilization and our values will survive nuclear war. If, on the other hand, one assumes that our government will continue to leave us defenseless and cannot be convinced to do otherwise, and if one assumes that nuclear war is inevitable and cannot be deterred, then all that is left is pessimism and emergency self-help.

By means of this approach, highly motivated individuals can save their own lives, at least for a short period during and after a nuclear attack. Unfortunately, only a small fraction of our people are likely to survive nuclear war through self-protection. This small fraction will not be able to preserve our territory or our values very long in the nuclear aftermath and will probably eventually perish.

Nevertheless, this book would not be complete without a few paragraphs about self-protection for civilians.

A family blast shelter along the lines described herein can be constructed at a one-of-a-kind cost of about $2,000 per person. It should be located under or very near the family home. The protection and habitability requirements are, of course, qualitatively the same as for the 150 person shelters. Crowded occupancy can be avoided in family shelters, which should have at least 10 to 20 square feet per person. Additional protection can be provided by locating the home itself in a remote, rural location.

This will require substantial commitments of time and money and perhaps substantial alterations in one's life.

It is important, however, not to make "survival" such a way of life that it detracts substantially from one's quality of life. Investment in nuclear war survival should be like buying an insurance policy. Spend the money, get the insurance, hope you'll not ever need the insurance, and then go on about your life. *Don't ruin your life by making fear of nuclear war a way of life.*

If no community shelter and no personal family shelter is built prior to nuclear attack, then there is still one last desperate action available. Procure a shovel, buy a copy of Cresson Kearny's *Nuclear War Survival Skills*, and hope and pray that the Soviets will be so foolish as to give you 24 to 48 hours' warning, follow the book's instructions, drive out into the country, and dig!

Most of you won't make it.

For the few million who might make it, however, the effort should provide some additional months of life. Maybe you can even find a way to fit into the tyranny that will come during the following years.

In any case, saved lives are saved lives, and the patriotic and dedicated scientists and engineers who developed these expedient survival techniques can be justly proud that they tried to save their country and at least saved a few of their countrymen.

Appendix 7

SOVIET TARGETS

In this book we use the worst possible Soviet nuclear attack in our primary arguments, because:

1. Since the Soviets are *capable* of this attack, we must be prepared for it.
2. The proposed shelter system will protect us even in this worst case.
3. America will still be a very desirable place to live even after such an attack, *if we have shelters*.

We must realize, however, that the nature of the Soviet attack will be determined by our defenses. The *worst case attack* will be used *only if we build no defenses*. If we build very good defenses, they will not attack at all. This is true in general, and is also true of particular targets if an attack comes.

For example, *our homes will be targets only if we are inside of them*. They want to kill us, not destroy our homes as such. The Soviets have always had a serious housing shortage, because they divert most of their productivity into building machinery for war. They would be very pleased to "inherit" our homes.

The Soviets have large groups of scientists working on a crash program to develop *biological weapons*. These weapons would have very little use against *military* targets. Their primary use would be the *extermination* of civilians *without* damage to civilian possessions like homes, automobiles, and industrial tools.

Since America can only be defeated if the people of America are destroyed, the Soviets will attempt to kill those people wherever they find them. If we are in our homes, our homes may be smashed in order to kill us. If we are in shelters, then there will be no reason to destroy our homes.

The best way to insure that any Soviet attack would be limited to military targets is to place our civilians beyond the reach of Soviet weapons.

In summary, the most probable Soviet nuclear attacks are:

1. In our current, completely undefended condition.

The Soviet attack would be a massive bombardment of our cities, towns, industry, and military targets. Ground bursts would be used against military and civilian airports and missile silos.

Fallout from these ground bursts and the effects of the air burst attack on our civilians would kill 80 to 90 percent of the American people.

2. If we *deploy* passive defense in the form of shelter now!

The Soviet attack might be deterred. If it came, it would be limited to ground bursts against airports and missile silos and air bursts against other military targets.

3. If we *deploy* shelters and *deploy* off-the-shelf anti-aircraft and anti-missile technology now!

The Soviet attack will be deterred until they build offensive weapons that can penetrate our anti-aircraft and anti-missile defenses.

4. If we *deploy* shelters, if we *deploy* off-the-shelf anti-aircraft and anti-missile technology now, and proceed with a serious program of advanced technology for strategic defense which is *deployed* as it becomes available (Star Shield or Star Wars).

The Soviets will never attack with nuclear weapons. War would only come by accident or by error. If, however, war did come, we would be safe. Even in an all out war, only a few targets in America might be damaged as a result of occasional defense leakage or terrorist infiltration.

In the age of biological weapons to come, our shelters would still help us. The filtered air and button-up capability would allow us to wait out a biological attack and to subdivide ourselves into one to two million separate biological targets.

Appendix 8

FUMBLING THE FOOTBALL: HOW THE MAD STRATEGY *REALLY* WORKED!!

This is the story of a football. Not Big Ten football — the Big One Football. The *Really* Big One.

The United States has what are called Emergency Actions Procedures. In case of a first strike by the Soviet Union on the U.S., the President has to respond before the first missiles hit: within 25 minutes for land-based ICBM's launched from the Soviet Union, and within perhaps 10 to 15 minutes for nearby submarine-launched missiles. Not much time, in other words.

Bill Gulley used to be in charge of seeing to it that the procedures that the President is to follow are coordinated. He worked for Presidents Johnson, Nixon, and Ford as a military liaison agent. He was a retired military man. He was the head of the Military Office at the White House under President Ford.

This brings us to the Football.

The Football is a manual, the White House

Emergency Procedures manual, WHEP for short. It's nicknamed the Football. The White House has a copy, and so does the Pentagon. It spells out exactly what steps the President must take to achieve a particular response by the military. Only it wasn't an "it"; it was a "they." The two manuals for years didn't agree with each other, and nobody knew it. Therein lies a tale, a tale of lies.

Upon confirmation that a launch has taken place (this must be confirmed, eating up precious time), the Pentagon Command Center signals the White House and the various military commands around the world.

When the operator at the White House military switchboard receives this alert, he sounds a claxon. The warrant officer with the Football is supposed to go to the President immediately. The warrant officer then opens the Football to get out the Black Book. The warrant officer has the combination; the President doesn't.

The President is supposed to be carried by helicopter to a nearby air base to board one of four huge flying electronic command posts, which is supposed to be ready for take-off by the time he arrives. Or he can be flown to one of eight sites, supposedly classified, but which the Soviets know all about. Of course, they're certainly targeted.

But what if the President isn't home? What if he's shooting the rapids somewhere, or whatever? The Soviets would know; they read the newspapers.

Or the President could go into a one-mile deep hole beneath the White House to protect himself.

Except that there isn't one. The Soviet premier has one, but the President doesn't.

In 1975, Donald Rumsfeld, the Secretary of Defense, tried out the system. He and the chairman of the Joint Chiefs of Staff scheduled a test. Rumsfeld picked up the phone on Gen. Brown's emergency telephone. He didn't get the President. He got someone on the White House signal board. Rumsfeld identified himself and asked to speak to the President.

Rumsfeld later claimed that he waited ten minutes. The operator insisted that it was only three. Rumsfeld finally asked what was taking so long. The answer: "I'm trying to find Kollmorgen," who was director of the Military Office. When Rumsfeld asked why he couldn't speak to the President, he was informed that he had to be cleared by Kollmorgen before he could speak to the President. But the operator couldn't find Kollmorgen.

Tough luck, Mr. Secretary of Defense. Also tough luck, for millions of Americans, had there been a real Soviet attack. As Gulley comments:

> So here you had a situation where the chairman of the Joint Chiefs of Staff, and the duty general in the Pentagon Command Center, believed all along—for many years—that all they had to do in a crisis was pick up that emergency phone and the President would immediately answer it. And it would not have happened.[1]

---

1. Bill Gulley, *Breaking Cover* (New York: Simon & Schuster, 1980). p. 185.

What had happened? One of Gulley's predecessors under Kennedy saw that there was no clear understanding of the Emergency Procedures. So he wrote up the procedures. He wanted to keep both the Pentagon and White House staff happy, so he wrote up two sets of instructions, with each group getting the set that made them important in the list of people to be notified. Then, in order to make his own office seem crucial, he wrote in a clearing role for himself which slowed down the whole alert: the person calling in had to be cleared by him.

Neither side ever knew that there were two different sets of instructions until Rumsfeld made his fateful call — over a decade later. When Gulley came in as the new officer, he made the changes. But they didn't help much, he said.

The President doesn't have the Football until the warrant officer brings it to him. The warrant officer knows what all the papers mean. The President never sees it beforehand. He could, of course, but he never asks, Gulley said. (Warrant officer, by the way, is a peculiar rank: above a sergeant but below a second lieutenant.) Whenever Jimmy Carter went to his hometown of Plains, Georgia for a visit, the aide with the Football stayed in a hotel room in Americus, ten miles down the road.[2]

Before Gulley, the Football was locked in a safe in a nearby bomb shelter, and only the warrant officer had the combination. There was no way for the warrant officer to get it to the President in time, if

---

2. *Ibid.*, p. 193.

the Soviets used a submarine-launched missile. Gulley said in 1980, "If the balloon ever did go up, it would be pure pandemonium." This was long after he made the system more efficient.

What if the enemy killed the President and Vice President in a coordinated attack? Gulley shows how easy it would be for a small terrorist group to get into the White House, let alone a KGB terrorist group. There will be no retaliation, unless the Soviets give us a warning for some reason as part of a particular strategy. It's their choice. Unless we had a protected President and foolproof communications, Gulley says, we could not retaliate. We have neither, he says, and it was his job to know.

So much for America's reigning nuclear war strategy, Mutual Assured Destruction. It is well-named: MAD.

Appendix 9

HOW CARTHAGE SOUGHT PEACE

The Romans and the Carthaginians battled for control of the Western world for over a century. They fought three major wars, called the Punic Wars: 264-241 B.C., 218-202 B.C., and 150-146 B.C.

When Carthage fell in 146 B.C., the Romans looted the city, killed most of the inhabitants, and salted over the land so that it could not grow crops again. This is the way of empires. Modern historians seem unable to understand Rome's actions against a weakened rival that posed no military threat to Rome. "It is difficult to understand these vindictive actions of Rome, apparently the product of childish or wanton rage."[1] Most modern American "Sovietologists" seem equally unable to understand why the Soviet Union is perfectly willing to imitate Rome's destruction of Carthage.

What is seldom found in modern history textbooks is the story of how the Romans first persuaded

---

1. Carl Roebuck, *The World of Ancient Times* (New York: Scribner's, 1966), p. 479.

the Carthaginian Senate to disarm its people. Two centuries ago, this was a well-known aspect of the Third Punic War. We find a classic recounting of the cowardice of the Carthaginian political leaders in a sermon preached by a minister in Rhode Island and sent to Bostonians in 1774, the summer after the famous "Boston Tea Party." The British had closed the Boston port as a punishment, and the Boston economy was in a depression. The Rhode Island minister reminded the Bostonians of what it can mean to surrender to a determined enemy. We reprint this document as a reminder of what the founders of the new American nation believed.

We are seeing a replay of Roman strangulation tactics in the grand strategy of the Soviet Union. We may be seeing a replay of the Carthaginian Senate's peace program in the not-so-grand strategy of the United States. We had better soon see a replay of Boston's resistance.

*　*　*　*　*

RHODE ISLAND, July 21, 1774 . . . to the worthy inhabitants of the Town of Boston — My Dear Brethren: The manly firmness with which you sustain every kind of Ministerial abuse, injury, and oppression, and support the glorious cause of liberty, reflects the highest honour upon the town. The few, very few amongst you, who have adopted the principles of slavery, serve, like the shade in a picture, to exhibit your virtues in a more striking point of light. Unhappy men, I sincerely pity them, that they should have so little sense of the dignity of human nature; so little sense of their duty to GOD, as to wish to reduce rational beings, formed after his divine image, to a state of brutish or worse than brutish servitude; that they should be so dead to all the feelings of humanity, public spirit, and universal benevolence, as to prefer the sordid pleasure of being upper slaves to foreign tyrants, and under them tyrannizing over their country, to the god-like satisfaction of saving that country.

How wretched these men mistake happiness! All the riches and honour in the world cannot give any pleasure in the least degree equal to the sincere heartfelt joy which the patriot feels in the consciousness of having supported the dignity, the freedom, and happiness of his country.

The attempt made by these men to annihilate your Committee of Correspondence was very natural. The robber does not wish to see our property entirely secured. An enemy, about to invade a foreign country, does not wish to see the coast well guarded and the country universally alarmed. Upon the same principles these men wish the dissolution of the Committee. They know that a design was formed to rob the Americans of their property; they hoped to share largely in the general plunder; but they now see that by the vigilance, wisdom, and fidelity, of the several Committees of Correspondence, the people are universally apprized of their danger, and will soon enter into such measures for the common security as will infallibly blast all their unjust expectations; and this is the true source of all the abuse thrown upon your Committee. But Oh, ye worthy few! continue to treat all their attempts with the neglect which they deserve. Thus the generous mastiff looks down with pity and contempt upon the little noisy, impertinent curs, which bark at him as he walks the street. Your faithful services have endeared you to the wise and good in every Colony. Continue your indefatigable labours in the common cause, and you will soon see the happy success of them in the salvation of your country.

The tools of power, and their connections, I imagine, are daily persuading you, my brethren, to submit to the Ministry. They pretend to pity your distresses, and assure you that the only way for you to get relief, is the making compensation for the tea, and submitting to the Revenue Acts. But did ever a man preserve his money by delivering up his purse to the highwayman who dared to demand it? Is it the way to preserve life, to throw away our arms and present our naked bosoms to the murderer's sword?

The town of Boston has been resembled to Carthage, and threatened with the same fate by a Member of Parliament. The execution of the sentence is already begun. It may not be amiss, then, to turn to the history of that people.

There had been two long and very bloody wars between Rome and that city. The Romans were victorious. But the Carthagenians having, in a few years, almost recovered their former state of wealth and power, the Romans looked upon them with a jealous eye, and took every opportunity (unless by an open war) to depress them. The Carthagenians, dreading a war, and hoping, by a proper submission, to conciliate the Roman affection, sent Ambassadors to Rome, with orders to declare that they entirely abandoned themselves, and all they possessed, to the discretion of the Romans.

The Senate of Rome, in return, granted them their liberty; the exercise of their own laws, all their territories and possessions, as private persons, or as a Republick, on condition that, in thirty days, they should send three hundred hostages to Lilybaeum, and do what the Consuls should order them.

This cruel order was submitted to. The hostages were immediately sent. They were the flower and hopes of the most noble families of Carthage. Upon their departure nothing was heard but the most dismal cries and groans; the whole city was in tears; and the mothers of these devoted youth tore their hair and beat their breasts in all the agonies of grief and despair. They fastened their arms around their lovely offspring, and could not be separated from them but by force. This cruel sacrifice, I should think, would have melted the Romans into compassion; but it had no such effect. Ambition and tyranny are incapable of any humane or tender feeling. The Deputies, therefore, attended the Roman camp, and told the Consuls they were come in the name of the Senate of Carthage, to receive their orders, which they were ready to obey in all things. The Consul praised their good disposition and ready obedience, and ordered them to deliver up all their arms. This fatal order was complied with, and an infinite number of weapons of all kinds, and a fine fleet of ships, accordingly delivered up.

Would any thing less than the entire destruction of Carthage have satisfied the Romans, they would now have been perfectly content. They had wholly disarmed the Carthagenians, and got all the noble youth hostages, as a security for their quiet submission; but all this did not satisfy them. The Consul sternly told them that the Senate of Rome had determined to destroy Carthage; that they must quit their city and remove to some other part of their territory, four leagues from the sea. This they refused to do.

The Romans therefore attacked their city, which, notwithstanding its defenseless state, bravely sustained a most terrible seige three whole years. Had the Carthagenians preserved their youth, the navy, and their arms; had they united their neighboring nations against the common oppressor, and immediately prepared for their defense, they might, perhaps, have defeated the Romans, and preserved their city entirely, or at least for many years longer. But they, by imprudent submissions put themselves wholly in the power of the enemy; and the consequences were, the miserable death of several hundred thousand people, and the utter destruction of their city! Take warning, my dear countrymen, by this terrible example. . . . [1]

---

1. Verna M. Hall (ed.), *The Christian History of the Constitution of the United States of America: Christian Self-government with Union* (San Francisco: Foundation for American Christian Education, [1962] 1969), pp. 536-539.

Appendix 10

PSALMS FOR PUBLIC WORSHIP IN A NATIONAL CRISIS

The average congregation probably isn't ready for the story of the military inferiority of the United States. National leaders continue to assure the American people that we are militarily strong. The facts are very different. But a pastor has an educating job to do before he introduces public prayers against the Soviet Union. These psalms and prayers, like the subject of unilateral assured destruction, are too far removed from the average congregation's experience.

Ignorance, however, does nothing for the country when the sirens sound. We cannot run into the streets and proclaim to everyone that we're sorry we were so foolish. There is a cure for ignorance: knowledge.

Here is what we recommend that pastors or elders do. They should take copies of this book to other officers of the local congregation. If a respected elder or pastor recommends that every church officer read this book, the others will read it. It has been written in such a way that it shouldn't take more than an evening or two for any informed person to read it. The facts are clear.

Once the other church officers have read the book, the pastor should call an officers' meeting to discuss it. If a majority is agreed, then they should all begin praying these prayers in their own private meetings. They should also pray that the congregations of every Bible-believing church have their hearts prepared for the message in this book.

Once several regular officers' meetings have included the suggested prayers at the end of the meetings, the officers should be ready to begin the next phase of the educational and motivational process. They should personally and quietly go to key members of the congregation and tell them of the elders' concern with this subject. A quiet, personal contact will give the quite accurate impression that this is serious. The member should be asked to read the book and sit down later on with the elder who gave it to him. The elder should try to gain some indication of the member's reaction.

If this is done steadily, the elders will gain the confidence of the key members of the church. They, in turn, should be encouraged to pass along this book to other members, and in the same way: face-to-face, quietly, with a request that the recipient get back to him within a week to discuss it.

Member by member, the seeds will be sown. Before the pastor goes before the congregation without warning to introduce the information in this book, he should do the necessary spade work. He needs to dig the ecclesiastical ground before he tells the story of digging the actual ground.

What is needed is a steady program of education and motivation. Members have to be told that this problem exists. For 30 years, the leaders of this nation have remained silent, so as not to arouse either the people of this nation or the Soviet General Staff.

There is not much time remaining. These facts must be put before the American people. But it will have to be told on a face-to-face basis primarily.

The authors of this book are convinced that the prayers of Bible-believing people are crucial to this nation's ability to escape what appears to be coming: defeat or destruction. We believe that prayers before God are more important than holes in the ground. We believe, however, that having both prayers and holes in the ground is best. But we must start with prayers. The prayers will help keep the Soviets confused, and also keep their fingers off the buttons until this nation has prepared itself for the worst.

The churches must be the pioneers in this reversal of American opinion. Their members are the largest group of people who are in a position to offer intercessory prayer for the nation, and also to pressure Congress to do something.

The pastors need not call for direct political action from the pulpit. All they need to do is to begin educating their congregations about the problem of military inferiority and the even greater problem of the lack of protection for the American people.

These prayers need to be prayed. So does a

variation of the prayer of Moses. We begin with what we have: access to God. We don't have a lot of direct political influence yet. We don't have a lot of political experience. But we do have access to God, and that is far more important than political experience.

The survival of the West depends now on the dedication and prayers of the churches. To get these prayers prayed, pastors and elders must begin to exercise responsibility. We are pricing bulk orders of this book to make it possible for pastors and elders to exercise this responsibility effectively and inexpensively. (See the tear-out sheet at the end of this book: **Ordering More Copies.**)

It is now up to the church leaders of this nation. If they refuse to do anything, or if they are unsuccessful in bringing this information to their congregations, then we might as well start counting the days until the catastrophe — the worst catastrophe in this nation's history, a catastrophe that may end this nation's history.

Psalm 83
(A Psalm of Condemnation)

1 Keep not thou silence, O God: hold not thy peace, and be not still, O God.

2 For lo, thine enemies make a tumult: and they that hate thee have lifted up the head.

3 They have taken crafty counsel against thy people, and consulted against thy hidden ones.

4 They have said, Come, and let us cut them off from *being* a nation; that the name of Israel may be no more in remembrance.

5 For they have consulted together with one consent: they are confederate against thee:

6 The tabernacles of Edom, and the Ishmaelites; of Moab, and the Hagerenes;

7 Gebal, and Ammon, and Amalek; the Philistines with the inhabitants of Tyre;

8 Assur also is joined with them: they have helped the children of Lot. Selah.

9 Do unto them as *unto* the Midianites; as *to* Sisera, as *to* Jabin, at the brook of Kison:

10 Which perished at Endor: they became *as* dung for the earth.

11 Make their nobles like Oreb, and like Zeeb: yea, all their princes as Zebah, and as Zalmunna:

12 Who said, Let us take to ourselves the houses of God in possession.

13 O my God, make them like a wheel; as the stubble before the wind.

14 As the fire burneth a wood, and as the flame setteth the mountains on fire;

15 So persecute them with thy tempest, and make them afraid with thy storm.

16 Fill their faces with shame; that they may seek thy name, O Lord.

17 Let them be confounded and troubled for ever; yea, let them be put to shame, and perish:

18 That *men* may know that thou, whose name

alone is JEHOVAH, *art* the most high over all the earth.

Psalm 91
(A Psalm of Dependence)

1 He that dwelleth in the secret place of the most High shall abide under the shadow of the Almighty.

2 I will say of the LORD, *He is* my refuge and my fortress: my God; in him will I trust.

3 Surely he shall deliver thee from the snare of the fowler, *and* from the noisome pestilence.

4 He shall cover thee with his feathers, and under his wings shalt thou trust: his truth *shall be thy* shield and buckler.

5 Thou shalt not be afraid for the terror by night; *nor* for the arrow *that* flieth by day;

6 *Nor* for the pestilence *that* walketh in darkness; *nor* for the destruction *that* wasteth at noonday.

7 A thousand shall fall at thy side, and ten thousand at thy right hand; *but* it shall not come nigh thee.

8 Only with thine eyes shalt thou behold and see the reward of the wicked.

9 Because thou hast made the LORD, *which is* my refuge, *even* the most High, thy habitation;

10 There shall no evil befall thee, neither shall any plague come nigh thy dwelling.

11 For he shall give his angels charge over thee, to keep thee in all thy ways.

12 They shall bear thee up in *their* hands, lest thou dash thy foot against a stone.

13 Thou shalt tread upon the lion and adder: the young lion and the dragon shalt thou trample under feet.

14 Because he hath set his love upon me, therefore will I deliver him: I will set him on high, because he hath known my name.

15 He shall call upon me, and I will answer him: I *will be* with him in trouble; I will deliver him, and honour him.

16 With long life will I satisfy him, and shew him my salvation.

BIBLIOGRAPHY

The following is an abbreviated bibliography of research reports and articles that, in part, served as the scientific background for this book. On each topic we have listed only a few references.

Most of these documents are available from the Emergency Technology Library (ETL) of the Oak Ridge National Laboratory (ORNL).

ORNL report number 6252, *Civil Defense Shelters —State of the Art Assessment* by C. V. Chester and G. P. Zimmerman, which is expected to be published in the fall of 1986, contains a definitive listing of the ORNL ETL references. We are indebted to Chester and Zimmerman and their co-workers for making this library available to us as well as the approximately 1,000 articles that they assembled for report 6252, and also their February 1986 draft of the report itself.

Many of these documents contain information important to several categories. We have, however, listed each only once.

Civil Defense in Other Countries

1. Goure, L., *Shelters in Soviet War Survival Strategy*, AD-A053250, prepared for the Defense Civil Preparedness Agency by the University of Miami, Center for Advanced International Studies, Coral Gables, FL, February 1978.

2. Cristy, G. A. (ed.), *Technical Directives for the Construction of Private Air Raid Shelters and the 1971 Conception of the Swiss Civil Defense* (TWP-1966, Swiss Federal Department of Justice and Police Office of Civil Defense—English Language Edition), ORNL-TR-2707, Oak Ridge National Laboratory, Oak Ridge, TN, 1973.

3. Akimov, N. I., *Civil Defense, Moscow 1969*, (translated from Russian by S. J. Rimshaw), ORNL-TR-2306, Oak Ridge National Laboratory, Oak Ridge, TN, April 1971.

4. Basic Military Knowledge Writing Group (China), *Chinese Civil Defense* (a translation from the Chinese of Chapter 7 and a part of Chapter 3; edited by C. V. Chester and C. H. Kearny), ORNL-TR-4171, Oak Ridge National Laboratory, Oak Ridge, TN, September 1974.

5. O'Brian, T., "A Survey of Civil Defence Measures in the Western Industrial Nations," *AEGIS International (Switzerland)* 3 (3), pp. 4-10, June/July 1984.

6. Korolev, V. I., (ed.), *What Everyone Must Know and be Able to Do (When Under Attack by Weapons of Mass Destruction)—Instructions for the Population*, FSTC-HT-268-84, translated from Russian for U.S. Army Foreign Science and Technology Center, Charlottesville, VA, June 1984.

7. *Chinese Civil Defense*, Protect and Survive Monthly, July 1981, pp. 32-33.

8. Titov, M. N., et al., *Civil Defense, Moscow 1974* (translated from Russian by Joint Publication's Research

Service, Arlington, VA; edited by G. A. Cristy),
ORNL-TR-2845, Oak Ridge National Laboratory,
Oak Ridge, TN, July 1975.

9. Egorov, P. T., I. A. Shlyakhov, and N. I. Alabin, *Civil Defense, Moscow 1970,* (Translated from Russian by Scientific Translation Service, Ann Arbor, MI; edited by J. S. Gailar, C. H. Kearny, and C. V. Chester) ORNL-TR-2793, Oak Ridge National Laboratory, Oak Ridge, TN, December 1973.

General Information

10. Galsstone, S., and P. J. Dolan (eds.) *The Effects of Nuclear Weapons* (Third Edition), published by the U.S. Department of Defense and the U.S. Department of Energy, 1977.

11. Mitchell, D. L., *An Optimization Study of Blast Shelter Deployment — Volumes I, II, and III,* LAMBDA Report 3; prepared for the Office of Civil Defense by the Institute for Defense Analysis, Arlington, VA, September 1, 1966.

12. Rockett, F. C., *A Low-Casualty Program of Hardened and Dispersed Shelters,* HI-685-P, Hudson Institute, Inc., Harmon-on-Hudson, NY, April 1966.

13. Krupka, R. A., et al., *Shelter Configuration Factors (Engineering and Cost Analysis),* AD-405709, prepared for the Office of Civil Defense by Guy B. Panero, Inc., New York, NY, April 1963.

14. Chester, C. V., and D. W. Holladay, *A Preliminary Study of Reducing the Cost of Blast Shelter for Critical Workers,* ORNL-5958, prepared for Federal Emergency Management Agency by Oak Ridge National Laboratory, Oak Ridge, TN, October 1983.

15. Haaland, C. M., C. V. Chester, and E. P. Wigner, *Survival of the Relocated Population of the U.S. After a Nuclear Attack* (Final Report), ORNL-5041, Oak Ridge Na-

National Laboratory, Oak Ridge, TN, June 1976.

16. Haaland, C.M. and Heath, M. T., *Mapping of Population Density*, ORNL-TM-4246, Oak Ridge National Laboratory, Oak Ridge TN, June 1983.

17. Haaland, C. M., E. P. Wigner and J. V. Wilson, *Active and Passive Defense Interaction Studies: Vol. 1 Summary, Models, and Calculations*, ORNL-TM-3485, Oak Ridge National Laboratory, Oak Ridge, TN, December 1971.

18. Chester, C. V., H. B. Shapira, G. A. Cristy, M. Schweitzer, S. A. Carnes, and D. Torri-Safdie, *Hazard Mitigation Potential of Earth-Sheltered Residences*, ORNL-5957, Oak Ridge National Laboratory, Oak Ridge, TN, November 1983.

19. Cohen, S. T., *We Can Prevent WWIII*, Jameson Books, Inc., Ottawa, IL, 1985.

20. Jastrow, R., *How To Make Nuclear Weapons Obsolete*, Little, Brown, Co., Boston, MA, 1985.

21. Forrestal, M. J., *Protection Against High Blast Overpressure and Ground Shock* (Final Report), MR-1188, prepared for Office of Civil Defense by General American Transportation Corporation, MRD Division, Niles, IL, February 28, 1963.

22. University of Arizona, *Cost Studies in Protective Construction Systems — General Studies in Costing Techniques with Specific Application to Shelter Systems for Tucson, Arizona, and Houston, Texas* (Final Report), Subcontract 138-4, prepared for Institute for Defense Analyses, by University of Arizona Engineering Research Laboratory, Tucson, AZ, January 1965.

23. University of Arizona, *Local Civil Defense Systems — A Study of Counterforce Defense Systems Methodology Applied to Tucson, Arizona and Environs* (Final Report), AD-6032-6, University of Arizona Engineering Research Laboratory, Tucson, AZ, June 4, 1964.

24. Waterman, G. S., *An Effective Shelter Program*, M59-100,

Industrial College of the Armed Forces, Washington, DC, April 1959.

25. Uher, R. A, *The Role of a Blast Shelter System in Strategic Defense*, ORNL-TM-2134, Oak Ridge National Laboratory, Oak Ridge, TN, January 1969.

26. Federal Emergency Management Agency, *Protective Construction — Nuclear Blast Resistant Design*, TR-20 (Vol. IV), Washington, DC, March 1985.

27. Haaland, C. M., "Offense-Defensive Cost Studies," pp. 29-34 in *Annual Progress Report — Civil Defense Research Project, March 1969 — March 1970*, ORNL-4566 (Part I), Oak Ridge National Laboratory, Oak Ridge, TN, April 1971.

28. Holmes and Narver, Inc., *Structural and Shielding Considerations in the Design of Hardened Facilities*, HN-183, prepared for the Defense Atomic Support Agency by Holmes and Narver, Inc., Los Angeles, CA, June 1965.

29. Hamberg, W. A., A. M. Salee, and R. H. Watkins, *Study of Tactical Movement Concepts and Procedures for Civil Defense Planning*, ORI-TR-210 (AD-421933), prepared for the Office of Civil Defense by Operations Research, Inc., Silver Springs, MD, August 1963.

30. Jane's Weapon Systems 1985 — 1986, 16th Edition, ed., Ronald T. Petty, Jane's Publishing Co., London, England.

World War II Bombing and Shelter

31. U.S. Strategic Bombing Survey, *Public Air Raid Shelters in Germany*, Report No. 154, Physical Damage Division, Germany, January 1947.

32. U.S. Strategic Bombing Survey, Effects of Nuclear Weapons on Hiroshima and Nagasaki, 1947.

33. U.S. Strategic Bombing Survey, Summary of Effects of Strategic Bombing on Germany, 1947.

34. Guy B. Panero, Inc., *Underground Installation — Foreign Installations*, prepared for U.S. Army Chief of Engineers, by Guy B. Panero, Inc., New York, NY, October 31, 1948.

35. Miller, C. F., *Firefighting Operations in Hamburg, Germany, During World War II: Excerpts from the Hamburg Fire Department Documents on the Air Attacks During World War II, Appendixes, 3, 4, and 5 and Photographs*. AD-753346, prepared for the Defense Civil Preparedness Agency by United Research Services, Inc., Burlingame, CA, April 1972.

36. Earp, K. F., *Deaths from Fire in Large Scale Air Attack — with special reference to the Hamburg Fire Storm*, CD/SA-28, Home Office, Scientific Advisor's Branch, Whitehall, Great Britain, April 1953.

37. Groves, L. R., Report of the Manhattan Project Atomic Bomb Investigating Group, Manhattan Engineer District, 1946.

38. Lynch, F. X., "Adequate Shelters and Quick Reactions to Warning," *Science 142*, pp. 665-667, 1963.

Shelter Tests with Nuclear Weapons

39. Corsbie, R. L., *AEC Communal Shelter Evaluation* (Operation Buster, Project 9.1b), WT-360, Atomic Energy Commission, Washington, DC, March 1952.

40. Federal Emergency Management Agency, *FEMA attack Environment Manual (Civil Preparedness Guide; Chapter 1: Introduction to Nuclear Emergency Operations)*, CPG-2-1A1, Washington, DC, May 1982.

41. Beck, C. (ed.), *Nuclear Weapons Effects Tests of Blast Type Shelters — A Documentary Compendium of Test Reports*, CEX-68.3, U.S. Atomic Energy Commission, Washington, DC, June 1969.

42. Cohen, E. and A. Bottenhofer, *Test of German Underground Personnel Shelters* (Operation Plumbbob, Project

30.7), WT-1454, Ammann and Whitney, New York, NY, June 1962.

43. Albright, G. H., J. C. LeDoux, and R. A. Mitchell, *Evaluation of Buried Conduits as Personnel Shelters* (Operation Plumbbob, Project 3.2), WT-1421, U.S. Department of the Navy, Bureau of Yards and Docks, Washington, DC, and U.S. Naval Civil Engineering Laboratory, Port Hueneme, CA, July 14, 1960.

44. Flathau, W. J., R. A. Breckenridge, and C. K. Wiehle, *Blast Loading and Response of Underground Concrete-Arch Protective Structures* (Operation Plumbbob, Project 3.1), WT-1420, U.S. Army Engineer Waterways Experiment Station, Vicksburg, MS, and U.S. Naval Civil Engineering Laboratory, Port Hueneme, CA, June 5, 1959.

45. Randall, P. A., *Damage to Conventional and Special Types of Residences Exposed to Nuclear Effects* (Operation Teapot, Project 31.1), WT-1194, Office of Civil and Defense Mobilization, Washington, DC, Federal Housing Administration, Washington, DC, and Housing Home Finance Agency, Washington, DC, April 12, 1961.

46. Cohen, E., and N. Dobbs, *Test of French Underground Personnel Shelters* (Operation Plumbbob, Project 30.6) WT-1453, Ammann and Whitney, New York, NY, June 1960.

47. Flynn, A. P., *F.C.D.A. Family Shelter Evaluation* (Operation Buster, Project 9.1a), WT-359, Federal Civil Defense Administration, Washington, DC, March 1952.

48. Williamson, R. A., and P. H. Huff, *Test of Buried Structural-Plate Pipes Subjected to Blast Loading*, (Operation PLUMBBOB, Project 34.3), WT-1474, Holmes and Narver, Inc., Los Angeles, CA, July 1961.

Shelter Tests with Chemical Explosions

49. Strode, J. D., Jr., et al., *Proceedings of the Misers Bluff*

Phase II Results Symposium 27-29 March 1979 (Volume II), POR-7013-2 (WT7013-2), Defense Nuclear Agency, Kirtland Air Force Base, NM, September 26, 1979b.

50. Petras, J. L., A. H. Hoffer, R. F. Worley, and K. C. Brown, *Donn Blast Test No. 1* (Misers Bluff Event II-II, Final Report), Donn Incorporated, Westlake, OH, March 1979b.

51. Petras, J. L., A. H. Hoffer, R. F. Worley, and K. C. Brown, *Donn Blast Shelter Test No. 2* (Misers Bluff Event II-II, Final Report), Donn Incorporated, Westlake, OH, March 1979a.

52. Cohen, E., E. Laing, and A. Bottenhofer, *Responses of Protective Vaults to Blast Loading* (Operation Plumbbob, Project 30.4), WT-1451, Ammann and Whitney, New York, NY, May 1962.

53. Albright, G. H., E.J. Beck, J. C. LeDoux, and R. A. Mitchell, *Evaluation of Buried Corrugated-Steel Arch Structures and Associated Components* (Operation Plumbbob, Project 3.3), WT-1422, U.S. Department of the Navy, Bureau of Yards and Docks, Washington, DC, and U.S. Naval Civil Engineering Laboratory, Port Hueneme, CA, February 28, 1961.

54. Reid, G. H., and R. M. Grayson, *Proceedings of the Mill Race Preliminary Results Symposium, 16-18 March 1982 (Volume II)*, DNA-POR-7073-2, Defense Nuclear Agency, Kirtland Air Force Base, NM, July 1982a.

Blast and Shock Effects

55. Kapil, A. L., *Blast Vulnerability of Shelter Supplies*, GARD Final Report 1518, prepared for Office of Civil Defense by General American Transportation Corporation, Research Division, Niles, IL, March 1972.

56. Getchell, J. V., and S. A. Kiger, *Vulnerability of Shallow-Buried Flat-Roof Structures: Foam HEST 5*, Technical Re-

port SL-80-7 (Report 3), U.S. Army Engineer Waterways Experiment Station, Vicksburg, MS, February 1981.

57. Harrenstein, H., et al., *Yielding Membrane Elements in Protective Construction* (Final Report), AD-625782, prepared for Office of Civil Defense by University of Arizona, Engineering Research Laboratory, Tucson, AZ, May 28, 1965.

58. Nash, P. T., W. E. Baker, E. D. Esparza, P. S. Westine, N. W. Blaylock, Jr., R. E. White, and M. G. Whitney, *"Do-It-Yourself" Fallout Blast Shelter Evaluation*, UCRL-15605 and SWRI-7531, prepared for the Federal Emergency Management Agency through Lawrence Livermore National Laboratory by Southwest Research Institute, San Antonio, TX, March 1984.

59. Edmunds, J. E., *Structural Debris and Building Damage Prediction Methods*, URS-686-5, prepared for Office of Civil Defense by URS Research Co., Burlingame, CA, June 1968.

60. Wilton, C., K. Kaplan, and B. L. Gabrielsen, *The Shock Tunnel: History and Results (Volumes I-V)*, SSI-7618-1 (AD-A055518), prepared for Defense Civil Preparedness Agency by Scientific Services, Inc., Redwood City, CA, February 1968.

61. Heugel, W. F., and D. I. Feinstein, *Shelter Evaluation Program* (Final Report), IITRI Project No. M6088, prepared for Office of Civil Defense by IIT Research Institute Technology Center, Chicago, IL, February 1967.

62. White, C. S., et al., *Biological Effects of Pressure Phenomena Occurring Inside Protective Shelters Following a Nuclear Detonation* (Operation TEAPOT, Project 33.1), WT-1179, Lovelace Foundation for Medical Education and Research, Albuquerque, NM, October 1956.

Blast and Shock Protection

63. Chilton, A. B., *Blast Pressure Leakage into Closed Structures Through Small Openings,* Technical Study No. 23, U.S.

Department of the Navy, Bureau of Yards and Docks, Washington, DC, February 1958.

64. Zimmerman, G. P., and C. V. Chester, *High Explosive Testing of a Corrugated Metal Blast Shelter with Membrane Blast Doors*, ORNL/TM-9289, Oak Ridge National Laboratory, Oak Ridge, TN, December 1984.

65. Coulter, G. A., *Blast Loading of Closure for Use on Shelters-II*, ARBRL-MR-03338, U.S. Army Ballistic Research Laboratory, Aberdeen Proving Ground, MD, February 1984.

66. Hughes-Caley, F., and R. Kiang, *Blast-Closure Valves* (Final Report), SRI Project 4949-211, prepared for Office of Civil Defense by Stanford Research Institute, Menlo Park, CA, August 1965.

67. Asplin, L. I., and W. L. Brooks, *Evaluation of the German Coarse Sand Filter* (Engineering Group Report), ENGR, No. 56, U.S. Army Chemical Biological-Radiological Engineering Group, Army Chemical Center, Chemical Center, MD, March 1963.

68. Chester, C. V., *Tests of the LUWA Blast Valve*, ORNL-TM-2796, Oak Ridge National Laboratory, Oak Ridge, TN, December 1969.

69. University of Arizona, *Proceedings of the Symposium on Soil-Structure Interaction, Tucson, Arizona, June 8-11, 1964,* AD-610549 sponsored by the Office of Civil Defense, prepared by the University of Arizona, Engineering Research Laboratory, Tucson, AZ, September 1964.

70. Newmark, N. M., and J. D. Haltiwanger, *Air Force Design Manual-Principles and Practices for Design of Hardened Structures*, AFSWC-TDR-62-138, prepared for Air Force Special Weapons Center by University of Illinois, Department of Civil Engineering, Urbana, IL, December 1962.

71. Luscher, U., *Behavior of Flexible Underground Cylinders*, AFWL-TR-65-99, prepared for the U.S. Air Force

Weapons Laboratory by Massachusetts Institute of Technology, Department of Civil Engineering, Cambridge, MA, September 1965.

72. Newmark, N. M., *Design of Openings for Buried Shelters,* Contract Report No. 2-67, U.S. Army Engineer Waterways Experiment Station, Vicksburg, MS, July 1963.

73. Libovicz, B. A., R. B. Neveril, and H. F. Behls, *Preproduction Prototype Package Ventilation Kit, Second Structural and Human Factors Test*, GARD-1278-4.2, prepared for Office of Civil Defense, by General American Transportation Corporation, General American Research Division, Niles, IL, August 1965.

74. Brown, D., *Blast Shelter Concept II* (Revised), published by the Donn Corporation, Westlake, OH, December 1978.

Initial Nuclear Radiation and Fallout

75. Defense Civil Preparedness Agency, *Shelter Design and Analysis — Fallout Radiation Shielding*, TR-20 (Vol. I), Washington, DC, February 1978 (includes Change 1).

76. Cain, V. R., *A Study of the Radiation Shielding Characteristics of Basic Concrete Structures at the Tower Shielding Facility*, ORNL-3464, Oak Ridge National Laboratory, Oak Ridge, TN, January 21, 1964.

77. LeDoux, J. C., *Nuclear Radiation Shielding Provided by Buried Shelters*, NCEL-TR-025, U.S. Naval Civil Engineering Laboratory, Port Hueneme, CA, October 1959.

78. Auxier, J. A., Z. G. Burson, R. L. French, F. F. Haywood, L. G. Mooney, and E. A. Straker, *Nuclear Weapon Free-Field Environment Recommended for Initial Nuclear Radiation Shielding Calculations*, ORNL-TM-3396, Oak Ridge National Laboratory, Oak Ridge, TN, February 1972.

79. Cain, V. R., C. E. Clifford, and L. B. Holland, *Measurements of Radiation Intensities in Vertical Concrete-Lined Holes and an Adjoining Tunnel at the Tower Shielding Facility*, ORNL-3513, Oak Ridge National Laboratory, Oak Ridge, TN, March 1964.

80. Defense Civil Preparedness Agency, *Shelter Design and Analysis, Volume 2: Protection Factor Estimator with Instructions*, TR-20 (Vol. 2) (Supersedes earlier versions), Washington, DC, February 1976.

Ventilation, Cooling, and Air Supply

81. Guy B. Panero, Inc., *Shelter Configuration Factors (Engineering and Cost Analyses)*, AD-405709, New York, NY, April 15, 1963.

82. Fabuss, B. M., and A. S. Borsanyi, *Self-Contained Generator for Shelter Use*, MRB-6024-F, prepared for the Office of Civil Defense by Monsanto Research Corporation, Everett, MA, October 1964.

83. Charanian, T. R., and J. D. Zeff, *Experimental Evaluation of Environmental Control Systems for Closed Shelters*, GATC Report MRD 1242-2530 General American Transportation Corporation, MRD Division, Niles, IL, July 1964.

84. Charanian, T. R., A. J. Glueckert, R. G. Barile, and J. D. Zeff, *Environmental Control Systems for Closed Underground Shelters*, GATC Report MR-1190-50, General American Transportation Corporation, MRD Division, Niles, IL, April 1963.

85. Kapil, A. L., H. M. Sitko, and J. M. Buday, *Ventilation Kits*, GARD Final Report 1477, prepared for Office of Civil Defense by General American Transportation Corporation, Research Division, Niles, IL, November 1969.

86. Humphreys C. M., A. Henschel, and D. H. K. Lee, *Sensible and Latent Heat Losses from Occupants of Survival*

Shelters, AD-648467, prepared for Office of Civil Defense through the Department of Health, Education, and Welfare by Occupational Health Research and Training Facility, Cincinnati, OH, December 1966.

87. Kearny, C. H., *How to Make and Use a Homemade, Large-Volume, Efficient Shelter-Ventilating Pump: The Kearny Air Pump*, ORNL-TM-3916, Oak Ridge National Laboratory, Oak Ridge, TN, August 1972.

88. Beck, E. J., Jr., *Gravity Ventilation of Protective Shelters*, NCEL-TN-471, U.S. Naval Civil Engineering Laboratory, Port Hueneme, CA, July 1963.

89. Franke, H., and J. Schultz, "Shelters and Their Ventilation," *AEGIS International (Switzerland) 2* (2), pp. 4-11, April/May 1983.

90. William, D. E., *Air Revitalization Unit for Sealed Survival Shelters*, Naval Civil Engineering Laboratory, TR-R 697, October 1970 and TN N-987 December 1968.

Fire and Carbon Monoxide

91. Earp, K. F., *Deaths from Fire in Large Scale Air Attack—with special reference to the Hamburg Fire Storm*, CD/SA-28, Home Office, Scientific Advisor's Branch, Whitehall, Great Britain, April 1953.

92. Broido, A., and A. W. McMasters, *Effects of Mass Fires on Personnel in Shelters*, Technical Paper No. 50, Pacific Southwest Forest and Range Experiment Station, Forest Service, USDA, Berkeley, CA, August 1960.

Occupancy and Overcrowding

93. Strope, W. E., H. S. Etter, R. A. Golbeck, R. H. Heiskell, and J. H. Sheard, *Preliminary Report on the Shelter Occupancy Test of 3-17 December 1959*, USNRDL-TR-418, U.S. Naval Radiological Defense Laboratory, San Francisco, CA, May 4, 1960.

94. Hannifan, D. T., W. N. Blockley, M. B. Mitchell, and

P. H. Strudwick, *Physiological and Psychological Effects of Overloading Fallout Shelters*, AD-420449, prepared for the Office of Civil Defense by Dunlap and Associates, Inc., Santa Monica, CA, April 1963.

95. Biderman, A. D., M. Louria, and J. Bacchus, *Historical Incidents of Extreme Overcrowding*, BSSR-354-5 (AD-609752), Bureau of Social Science Research, Inc., Washington, DC, March, 1963.

Expedient Shelter

96. Kearny, C. H., *Nuclear War Survival Skills*, ORNL-5037, Oak Ridge National Laboratory, Oak Ridge, TN, September 1979.

97. Kearny, C. H. and C. V. Chester, *Blast Tests of Expedient Shelters* (Middle North Series, MIXED COMPANY Event; POR-6749; Final Project Officers Report—LN316) ORNL-4905, Oak Ridge National Laboratory, Oak Ridge, TN, January 1974.

98. Kearny, C. H., *Expedient Shelter Construction and Occupancy Experiments* ORNL-5039, Oak Ridge National Laboratory, Oak Ridge, TN, March 1976.

99. Kearny, C. H., and C. V. Chester, *Blasts of Expedient Shelters in the DICE THROW Event*, ORNL-5347, Oak Ridge National Laboratory, Oak Ridge, TN, March 1978.

Industrial Equipment Protection

100. Funston, N. E., T. H. Woo, and E. N. York, *Expedient Blast Shelters Employing Soil*, Boeing Corporation, Seattle, Washington.

101. Russel, J. W., and E. N. York, "Expedient Industrial Protection from Nuclear Attack, *"Practical Civil Defence*, No. 8, pp. 13-32 (May/June 1984).

102. Guy B. Panero, Inc., *Underground Installations* (Summary), Contract W-49-129-ENG-59, prepared for the U.S. Army Chief of Engineers by Guy B. Panero,

Inc., New York, NY, October 1948.

103. Russel, J. W. and E. N. York, *Expedient Industrial Protection Against Nuclear Attack*, Boeing Corporation, Seattle Washington, March 1980.

Food and Medicine

104. Franz, K. B., and C. H. Kearny, *Maintaining Nutritional Adequacy During a Prolonged Food Crisis*, ORNL-5352, Oak Ridge National Laboratory, Oak Ridge, TN, August 1979.

105. Klinghoffer, M., *Triage Emergency Care Book*, Technomic Publishing Co., Lancaster, Pennsylvania, 1985.

106. Cain, H. D., *Flint's Emergency Treatment and Management*, Seventh Edition, W. B. Saunders, Philadelphia, Pennsylvania, 1985.

Wells and Water

107. Guy B. Panero, Inc., *Shelter Configuration Factors (Engineering and Cost Analyses)*, AD-405709, New York, NY, April 15, 1963.

108. Guy B. Panero, Inc., *Cost Effectiveness of Water Wells* (Final Report), AD-447991, New York, NY, September 7, 1974.

109. Flanigan, F. M. and J. O. Gonzalez, Jr., *Moisture in Survival Shelters* (Final Report), AD-600437, prepared for Office of Civil Defense by University of Florida, Engineering and Industrial Experiment Station, Gainesville, FL, April 1964.

110. Hahl, R. G., *Manually Powered Pumping Equipment*, AD-403824, U.S. Army Engineer Research and Development Laboratories, Fort Belvoir, VA, October 15, 1962.

Furniture and Toilets

111. Kearny, C. H., *Shelter Furnishings for Efficient Living*

Space, ORNL-TM-1428, Oak Ridge National Laboratory, Oak Ridge, TN, March 1966.

112. Gates, J. W., and R. M. Schwaner, *Low-Cost Sleeping Facility* (Final Report), Civil Defense Project No. 1310, Quartermaster Research and Engineering Center, Natick, MA, October 1962.

113. Des Rosiers, P. E., *Investigation of Low-Cost Sanitation Systems*, USAERDL Project 8A72-04-001-29, U.S. Army Engineer Research and Development Laboratories, Fort Belvoir, VA, November 19, 1962.

114. Des Rosiers, P. E., *Human Waste Studies in an Occupied Civil Defense Shelter* (Division Report), AD-671703, U.S. Army Engineer Research and Development Laboratories, Fort Belvoir, VA, June 1965.

Power and Lights

115. General Electric Company, *Improvised Power Supplies* (Final Report), AD-445845, prepared for the Office of Civil Defense by the General Electric Company, Military Communications Department, Syracuse, NY, June 1964.

116. Office of Civil Defense, *Shelter Design and Analysis (Volume 3 - Environmental Engineering for Shelters)*, TR-20 (vol. 3), Washington, DC, May 1969.

117. Jago, A. G., and A. L. Kapil, *Lighting Kit*, GARD Final Report 1508, prepared for the Office of Civil Defense by General American Transportation Corporation, Niles, IL, September 1970.

Excavation and Tunnels

118. De Leuw, Cather and Company, *Deep Excavation Techniques for Shelters in Urban Areas (Preliminary Planning and Cost Data)*, AD-411786, prepared for Office of Civil Defense by De Leuw, Cather and Company, Chicago, IL, July 1963.

119. Viecelli, J., *Air Blast Protection in Tunnels*, UCRL-14848-T, Lawrence Radiation Laboratory, Livermore, CA, March 1966.
120. Baschiere, R. J., B. A. Humphreys, K. E. McKee, and E. Vey, *Evaluation of Deep Tunnel Shelters* (Final Report), ARF Project No. K149 (AD-276484), prepared for Office Civil and Defense Mobilization by Armour Research Foundation of Illinois Institute of Technology. Technology Center, Chicago, IL, November 1958.
121. Cristy, G.. A., Harrington, F. E., and McClain, W. C., Urban Research, 1. *Systems Analysis of Tunneling*, 1969.
122. Fass, H., *Vietcong Survivor Recalls Agony of Tunnel War*, New York Times, October 13, 1977.

Chemical and Biological Weapons Protection

123. Westinghouse Electric Corporation, *Development of a Specification for a 75 CFM Gas Particulate Filter Unit for Removing the CBR Contaminants of Warfare from the Air Supplied to Family Shelters* (Final Report), AD-296236 prepared for Army Chemical Center by Westinghouse Research Laboratories, Pittsburgh, PA, September 17, 1962.
124. Chester, C. V., and G. P. Zimmerman, "Civil Defense Implications of Biological Weapons—1984" *Journal of Civil Defense, 17 6-12*, (December 1984).

ABOUT THE AUTHORS

Arthur Robinson is a chemist. He did his undergraduate work at the California Institute of Technology (CalTech). He received his Ph.D. from the University of California at San Diego. He has worked primarily on the problems of the molecular biology of aging and preventive medicine.

Gary North received his Ph.D. in history from the University of California at Riverside, having specialized in Colonial American economic history and economic thought. He has worked with three nonprofit educational foundations in the field of economics and economic history. He also served as the research assistant for a U.S. Congressman. At present, Gary North is publisher of several newsletters and about twenty books.

ACKNOWLEDGMENTS

We express our thanks to the many scientists and engineers who provided facts to us for this book. We also thank the 1,900 readers of Remnant Review whose comments about the draft manuscript improved the text. Timely publication was made possible by the special effort of the editors, typists, typesetters, printers, and others to whom we are grateful.

SCRIPTURE INDEX

INDEX

FIGHTING CHANCE NEWSLETTER

Fighting Chance
P.O. Box 1279
Cave Junction, OR 97523

Gentlemen:

I read about your organization in the book *Fighting Chance*. I would like to receive your newsletter for civil defense information, including shelter designs, strategic news, and political action efforts.

Enclosed is $35 for a charter subscription for the first 12 issues of the newsletter. (Normal subscription price is $60.)

_____
name

_____
address

_____
city, state, zip

_____
telephone

UNCONDITIONAL SURRENDER

Dominion Press
P.O. Box 8204
Ft. Worth, TX 76124

Gentlemen:

I would like to order _____ copies of Gary North's simply written, 264 page introduction to Christian Theology, *Unconditional Surrender*. I am enclosing $9.95 for each copy.

_____
name

_____
address

_____
city, state, zip

_____
telephone

Call Toll-Free to charge your order:
1-800-527-8608
In Texas, collect, at 817-595-2691

RECOMMENDED BOOKS

Dominion Press
P.O. Box 8204
Ft. Worth, TX 76124

Gentlemen:

I read about your organization in the book *Fighting Chance*. Please send information on other publications by Gary North that may be of interest to me.

_____

name

_____

address

_____

city, state, zip

_____

telephone

MORE INFORMATION

Fighting Chance
P.O. Box 1279
Cave Junction, OR 97523

Gentlemen:

I am concerned about the nuclear threat and would like to receive information in the future about problems and solutions discussed in *Fighting Chance*.

Please send future information to me.

_____
name

_____
address

_____
city, state, zip

_____
telephone

FRAUDS IN YOUR LIFE

The following myths about nuclear war are fraudulent:

1. Legions of mutant children from increased back ground radiation.

2. Tens of millions of cancer victims from increased background radiation.

3. Nuclear Winter

4. "On the Beach" Syndrome — the earth will be uninhabitable.

These are dangerous myths. They help to keep us defenseless by causing a paralyzing fear among the American people. These myths, through promoting weakness, have greatly increased the danger of nuclear war.

If you would like the facts that refute these frauds, send $5 to: **Frauds, *Fighting Chance,*** P.O. Box 8204, Fort Worth, Texas 76124.

Name_____

Address_____

City/State/Zip_____

Telephone_____

DEAR SENATOR

Senator _____
Senate Office Bldg.
Washington, D.C. 20515

Dear Senator_____:

I am very concerned about the lack of any civil defense system for U.S. citizens. Red China has one, the Soviet Union has one, and Switzerland has one. We don't.

I want to know if you plan to support legislation for the immediate construction of a civil defense shelter system along the lines described in the book, *Fighting Chance*, by Arthur Robinson and Gary North.

If you don't intend to support such legislation, I would like to know why not. If your objection is that it costs too much, I would like to know which programs you regard as more important than protecting the lives of this nation's population from Soviet attack.

Sincerely yours,

_____

Name_____

Address_____

City/State/Zip_____

Telephone_____

DEAR SENATOR

Senator_____
Senate Office Bldg.
Washington, D.C. 20515

Dear Senator _____:

I am very concerned about the lack of any civil defense system for U.S. citizens. Red China has one, the Soviet Union has one, and Switzerland has one. We don't.

I want to know if you plan to support legislation for the immediate construction of a civil defense shelter system along the lines described in the book *Fighting Chance*, by Arthur Robinson and Gary North.

If you don't intend to support such legislation, I would like to know why not. If your objection is that it costs too much, I would like to know which programs you regard as more important than protecting the lives of this nation's population from Soviet attack.

Sincerely yours,

_____

Name_____

Address_____

City/State/Zip_____

Telephone_____

DEAR CONGRESSMAN

Congressman_____
House Office Bldg.
Washington, D.C. 20515

Dear Congressman _____:

I am very concerned about the lack of any civil defense system for U.S. citizens. Red China has one, the Soviet Union has one, and Switzerland has one. We don't.

I want to know if you plan to support legislation for the immediate construction of a civil defense shelter system along the lines described in the book *Fighting Chance*, by Arthur Robinson and Gary North.

If you don't intend to support such legislation, I would like to know why not. If your objection is that it costs too much, I would like to know which programs you regard as more important than protecting the lives of this nation's population from Soviet attack.

Sincerely yours,

_____

Name_____

Address_____

City/State/Zip_____

Telephone_____

ORDERING MORE COPIES

American Bureau of Economic Research
P.O. Box 8204
Ft. Worth, TX 76124

Gentlemen:

I would like to order additional copies of *Fighting Chance*.

Please send me:

_____ 5 copies for $10

_____ 10 copies for $15

_____ 50 copies for $50 (1 case)

_____ 1000 copies for $500 (20 cases)

I understand that these prices are postage paid bulk rate mail or U.P.S., except for 20 case quantities (freight paid by recipient). I enclose prepayment for the order.

_____
name

_____
address

_____
city, state, zip

_____
telephone